"One of the most comprehensive and insightful how-to's out there. *Save the Cat!* is a must-read for both the novice and the professional screenwriter."
> — Todd Black, Producer, *The Weather Man, S.W.A.T,*
> *Alex and Emma, Antwone Fisher*

"Want to know how to be a successful writer in Hollywood? The answers are here. Blake Snyder has written an insider's book that's informative — and funny, too."
> — David Hoberman, Producer, *The Shaggy Dog* (2005),
> *Raising Helen, Walking Tall, Bringing Down the House, Monk* (TV)

"This just may be the BEST book you'll ever need, or read, on the subject of how to break into the big screen big time. Snyder is a working, selling writer himself, so he gives the reader a true inside glimpse into what it's like, what it takes, and what to expect on the long road to screenwriting stardom. Many screenwriting how-to tomes are written by guys and gals who have few or no real studio credits, so with this book you can be sure you are getting the info direct from the source of a successful member of the Hollywood elite. This is no doubt the one book that will do more to help you achieve success and get your two-brad-bound puppy through the door than any other I've read so far. And believe me, folks, I've read them all."
> — Marie Jones, *www.AbsoluteWrite.com*

"You'd have to look far and wide to find a better book to help you achieve your goals. Quite simply one of the most practical guides to writing mainstream spec scripts on the market."
> — *Screentalk* Magazine

"Blake Snyder's *Save the Cat!* could also be called *Save the Screenwriter!*, because that's exactly what it will do: Save the screenwriter time, save the screenwriter frustration, and save the screenwriter's sanity. Blake takes you behind the scenes and into the decision-makers' offices as he explains how the Hollywood system works and what writers should do and expect as they journey through the perilous maze of Hollywood."
> — Andy Cohen, Literary Manager/Producer; President,
> Grade A Entertainment

"Shockingly informative, stunningly funny — I wish I'd had *Save the Cat!* to read when I was just starting out. It would have saved time, tears, and trees."
> — Susan Jansen, Writer-Producer, *The Lizzie McGuire Movie*, *Maybe This Time* (TV), *Boy Meets World* (TV); Writer, *Home Improvement* (TV)

"*Save the Cat!* offers the insight and knowledge needed to write and sell screenplays in today's competitive marketplace. Fun, fresh, and informative. Way to go, Blake!"
> — Valarie Phillips, Head of Motion Picture Literary, Paradigm Agency

"Blake is one of the brightest and most original thinkers in screenwriting today. His how-to approach is Grade-A, rock-solid advice."
> — Craig Baumgarten, Producer, *Peter Pan*, *Shattered Glass*

"As an executive I always looked for a way to fix an existing screenplay. And now, as a producer, I need a way to conceptualize as quickly and efficiently as possible — and Blake Snyder's insightful book is it!"
> — Kathryn Sommer Parry, Producer, *The Marine* (2005); Development Executive, *Basic Instinct*, *Rambo*, *Terminator 2*, *Chaplin*, *12 Monkeys*, *I Spy*

"Imagine what would happen in a town where more writers approached screenwriting the way Blake suggests? My weekend read would dramatically improve, both in sellable/producible content and in discovering new writers who understand the craft of storytelling and can be hired on assignment for ideas we already have in house. *Save the Cat!* is like a Berlitz guide to interpreting the secret language of every studio exec and producer in town. Once you learn to think like the people with the checkbook, you're one step closer to success."
> — From the Foreword by Sheila Hanahan Taylor, Vice President, Development at Zide/Perry Entertainment

SAVE THE CAT!

The Last Book on Screenwriting You'll Ever Need

BLAKE SNYDER

Published by Michael Wiese Productions
3940 Laurel Canyon Blvd. # 1111
Studio City, CA 91604
tel. (818) 379-8799
fax (818) 986-3408
mw@mwp.com
www.mwp.com

Cover Design: Michael Wiese Productions
Book Layout: Gina Mansfield
Editor: Brett Jay Markel

Printed by Sheridan Books, Inc., Chelsea, Michigan
Manufactured in the United States of America

Library of Congress Cataloging-in-Publication Data

Snyder, Blake, 1957-
  Save the cat! : the last book on screenwriting you'll ever need / Blake Snyder.
      p. cm.
  Includes index.
  ISBN 1-932907-00-9
  ISBN 978-1-932907-00-1
  1. Motion picture plays--Technique. 2. Motion picture authorship. I. Title: Last book on screenwriting you'll ever need. II. Title.
  PN1996.S65 2005
  808.2'3--dc22   2004009134

Printed on recycled stock

TABLE OF CONTENTS

ACKNOWLEDGMENTS

Of the many people who helped make this book a reality, I would first of all like to thank my friend and mentor, B. J. Markel, for both giving me wise counsel about the entertainment business and doing such a patient and sterling job in the editing of this book. I would also like to thank Ken Lee for his continuing support and enthusiasm, and Gina Mansfield, a true collaborator and artist. And most of all, I want to thank Michael Wiese, who has created such a winning brand of books about every aspect of the film industry, and is also one of its most proactive and successful participants. Finally, thanks for the encouragement I received from the gang "in and out of these rooms," especially Marin, Melanie, Rich, Lee, Lisa, Zed, Zak, Eric, Jake, and Wendell. Trudge on!

FOREWORD

By Sheila Hanahan Taylor, Producer at Zide/Perry Entertainment, whose films include the *American Pie* trilogy, *Hellboy*, *Cats and Dogs*, *Final Destination*, *Final Destination 2*; Associate Professor, UCLA Producer's Program.

With the turn of EVERY page of this book, I found myself using all of Blake Snyder's tools, hints, and ideas to double- and triple-check my own projects that are set up and in development at studios all over town! I love the idea that Blake has written a book that everyone can use — from the novice to the practicing producer. How often does that happen?!

I also found myself trying to come up with a way I could politely refer *Save the Cat!* to a number of repped, produced writers who could use a little goose from its tactics. Imagine what would happen in a town where more writers approached screenwriting the way Blake suggests? My weekend read would dramatically improve, both in sellable/produceable content and in discovering new writers who understand the craft of storytelling and can be hired on assignment for ideas we already have in house. (On second thought, are you SURE you want this published, Blake? It might beef up the competition!)

I've been searching for a book that masterfully uses the kind of "successful" examples studio heads use (*Miss Congeniality*, *Die Hard*, *Legally Blonde*, *Signs*) and peeks behind the curtain to explain them on all fronts — genre, plot, structure, marketing, casting — in a way that rookies and pros alike will understand and hopefully put to use. *Save the Cat!* is like a Berlitz guide to interpreting the secret language of every studio exec and producer in town. Once you learn to think like the people with the checkbook, you're one step closer to success.

I'm not exaggerating when I say at Zide/Perry — one of the premier homes for breaking new screenwriters and launching careers — we recommend every single one of Blake's strategies... from watching movies in the appropriate genre and breaking down all their key elements, to asking what the poster/who the cast is, to showing how using similar films as a benchmark is just good storytelling. When I picked up *Save the Cat!* it was like Blake had been in our offices for the last six years, hearing our words and recording them in a master bible.

Experience shows that following the steps in *Save the Cat!* works. I can name dozens of writers/producers who have launched their careers using the philosophy described on these pages! It's invaluable. Thank God, Blake has taken the time to put it all down in one efficient and witty place. And just like good exposition, the breezy writing here makes the instruction and insight sneak up on you. Before you know it, you've read the whole thing, learned a ton, and are still inspired to tackle your next project.

Because this book explores the craft of screenwriting starting from the business side of things, I consider it both essential and revolutionary. *Save the Cat!* takes into account both halves of the whole, for the route to success in this business is to strike a balance between art and commerce, and this book has done exactly that!

Just like my invaluable collection of classic, great scripts, *Save the Cat!* is a book to have on the shelf, right next to Syd Field's. I would absolutely revisit it whenever I find myself wanting a quick refresher course on commercial screenplay structure and strategy.

A final word: After reading dozens of how-to books, this is the FIRST book on screenwriting/the business that I've EVER asked the co-chairs at UCLA to consider making required reading. In fact, *Save the Cat!* is, to me, a must-read for anyone who is even remotely interested in being in the game.

INTRODUCTION

Another book on screenwriting!?

I'm sure that's what many of you are thinking.

And to an extent, you're right. There are lots of good screen writing how-to's out there. And if you want to see where it all began, look to the master, Syd Field, who started it all and taught everybody.

There are other really good books and courses, too, many of which I've sampled.

I like Viki King's book with the improbable title of *How to Write a Movie in 21 Days.* Improbable, yes, but I've done it — and sold the script I wrote, too.

I also value Joseph Campbell's work. *Hero With A Thousand Faces* remains the best book about storytelling ever.

And of course I have a soft spot for Robert McKee — for the value of his class performance if nothing else. McKee is like John Houseman in *The Paper Chase,* and if you're an aspiring screen-writer, you have to take at least one seminar from him. It's too great a piece of theater to miss.

Finally, for anyone who's watched lots of movies and seen enough bad ones to think "I can do THAT!" you may assume you don't need a "how-to-write-a-screenplay" book at all.

So why this one?

Why now?

And why can *I* tell you things you've never heard anywhere else that will make a difference in your script?

To begin with, what I've never seen out there is a book on screen-writing that "talks the way we talk." As a working professional in the entertainment industry, since I was eight doing voice work for my Dad, I'm used to a certain slangy shorthand when it comes to discussing the business. These books are all so academic! So ster-ile. They treat the movies with waaaaaay too much awe and respect — they're just movies! — and I think that gets in the way. Wouldn't it be nice if a book about how to write a screenplay used the kind of shorthand that screenwriters and movie executives use?

Secondly, and this is no slight against anyone, but I think it would be nice if the guy writing the book on how to write a screenplay had actually sold something! *Don't you think?* And this is an area where I feel particularly qualified. I have been a working screen-writer for 20 years and made millions of dollars doing it. I've sold lots of high concept, bidding war, spec screenplays. I've even had a couple made.

I've gotten script notes from Steven Spielberg, Michael Eisner, Jeffrey Katzenberg, Paul Maslansky, David Permut, David Kirschner, Joe Wizan, Todd Black, Craig Baumgarten, Ivan Reitman, and John Landis. And I've received the collective wisdom of many others — less famous but equally wise — that we all use, and like, and base our screenplays on.

Thirdly, wouldn't it be a bonus if the guy writing the how-to had actually used this method in the trenches by teaching others, *who actually go on to sell scripts?*

Well, that's me, too.

I've had a long track record of working with other screenwriters. I've taught my method and shortcuts to some of the most successful in the business. I've helped make them better screenwriters. It's because my approach to the task is practical, based on common sense — and mostly because it works.

And lastly, I think it would be good if a screenwriting book told you the truth about your chances of selling. There are tons of seminars and screenwriting programs out there that seem designed to encourage people and ideas that should not be encouraged. I don't know about you, but I find this cruel. Advice like: "Follow your heart!" and "Be true to your vision!" is fine if you're in therapy. Me? I really want to improve my odds. Life is short. I don't need to be misled into thinking my script based on the life of St. Aloysius or a "true-life event" that happened to me at camp one summer actually has a chance if it doesn't.

So why another screenwriting book? Because the others I've seen don't say it like it is, and don't give the reader the tools to attain success in the field. And on top of that, they often serve the writer of the book more than the reader. I personally don't want a career teaching screenplay writing courses; I just want to pass along what I know. And besides all that, I'm at the point when I'm ready to "give it away." I've had a lot of amazing breaks, I've learned from the masters, and now it's time for me to tell you.

I also undertook the writing of this book because of the lack of common sense I see in many of the movies that get made today. For all the knowledge out there, many in Hollywood forget the basics and ignore what works, thinking that just because they have studio offices and big expense accounts, they don't need to follow the rules anymore.

And, frankly, this drives me up a tree!

As I am writing this book, there is one phenomenon in particular that really bothers me, and yet from a business point of view it's pretty smart. It's the Make-Sure-It-Opens-Or-Else trend. This is where you spend a lot of money on the movie, hype the bejeezus out of it, open wide at 3,000+ theaters, and have a huge first weekend to recoup your cost. And who cares if your movie drops 70% or 80% in its *second* weekend because of bad word-of-mouth?

What bugs me about this trend is that for all the money they're spending on star salaries, special effects, advertising, and market-ing — and don't forget all those prints — it would be better spent, and the movies would be better too, if the filmmakers just paid $4 for some paper and pencils and *followed the rules of how to write a good movie!*

Take a hip, slick movie like *Lara Croft 2* for example. They spent a fortune on that film. And everyone is still wondering what hap-pened. They can't figure out why they didn't bring in the audience of targeted men. It's not surprising to me. What's wrong with this picture? Where did the filmmakers go awry? To me it's really very simple: I don't like the Lara Croft character. Why would I? She's cold and humorless. And while that's fine in the solitary world of video games and comics, it doesn't make me want to leave my home to go see the movie. The people who produced this film think they can get you to like her by making her "cool." This is what amounts to "character development" in *au currant* movies: *"She drives a cool car."* That's someone's idea of how to create a winning hero.

Well, folks, I don't care about how "cool" it is, this isn't going to work.

Why?

Because liking the person we go on a journey with is the single most important element in drawing us into the story.

Which brings us to the title of this book: *Save the Cat!*

Save the what?

I call it the "Save the Cat" scene. They don't put it into movies anymore. And it's basic. It's the scene where we meet the hero and the hero *does* something — like saving a cat — that defines who he is and makes us, the audience, like him.

In the thriller, *Sea of Love*, Al Pacino is a cop. Scene One finds him in the middle of a sting operation. Parole violators have been lured by the promise of meeting the N.Y. Yankees, but when they arrive it's Al and his cop buddies waiting to bust them. So Al's "cool." (He's got a cool idea for a sting anyway.) But on his way out he also does something nice. Al spots another lawbreaker, who's brought his son, coming late to the sting. Seeing the Dad with his kid, Al flashes his badge at the man who nods in understanding and exits quick. Al lets this guy off the hook because he has his young son with him. And just so you know Al hasn't gone totally soft, he also gets to say a cool line to the crook: "Catch you later..." Well, I don't know about you, but I *like* Al. I'll go anywhere he takes me now and you know what else? I'll be rooting to see him win. All based on a two second interaction between Al and a Dad with his baseball-fan kid.

Can you imagine if the makers of *Lara Croft* 2 spent $4 on a good Save the Cat scene instead of the $2.5 million they spent developing that new latex body suit for Angelina Jolie? They might've done a whole lot better.

That's why the name of this book is *Save The Cat!* It's emblematic of the kind of common sense basics I want to get across to you, and to some in the movie business, about the laws of physics that govern good storytelling. These are lessons my writing partners and I have learned through the real school of Hollywood hard knocks.

We, and hopefully you, are in the business of trying to pitch our wares to the majors, make a big sale, and appeal to the biggest possible audience. We want a hit — and a sequel if we can! Why play the game if you don't swing for the fence? And while I love the Indie world, I want to hit it out of the park in the world of the major studios. That's why this book is primarily for those who want to master the mainstream film market.

None of these rules, and none of my experiences in screenwriting, were discovered in a vacuum. I learned from all my writing partners to whom I dedicate this book: Howard Burkons, Jim Haggin, Colby Carr, Mike Cheda, Tracey Jackson, and Sheldon Bull. I also learned from, and owe my career to, my agents — like my beloved Hilary Wayne, my manager Andy Cohen, and many others. I have also been enlightened by my seminar students and Web writers, those who grew up loving the Indie film world, and who have given me new perspectives by questioning me in that snotty-as-hell 'tude that only insightful young people have.

If my Save the Cat example has whetted your appetite to learn more tricks, then let's begin. Because it's one of many that are basic. And they work.

Every time.

They're the rules I hope you will learn and use and even break. And hopefully when your movie comes out, and it's satisfying *and* a hit — you can pass on *your* rules to others.

1 WHAT IS IT?

We've all had this experience...

It's Saturday night.

You and your friends have decided to see a movie.

One of you is picked to read the choices from the newspaper while the others listen and decide. And if you are an aspiring spec screenwriter, you're about to learn a very important lesson.

If you've ever had the honor, if you've ever been the one elected to read the film choices for a group of gathered friends, congratulations, you have now had the experience of "pitching" a movie — just like the pros. And just like the pros, you have been faced with the same problem. Yes, the film stars George Clooney; sure, it's got amazing special effects; of course, Ebert and Roeper give it two thumbs up.

But what's it about?

If you can't answer that question, you know it pretty quickly. If what the movie is about isn't clear from the poster and the title, what are you going to say to describe it? Usually what you're left with, standing there, newspaper in hand, is telling your friends everything about the movie that it's *not*. What you heard. What *People* Magazine said. Some cockeyed re-telling of the plot that the star revealed on *Letterman*. And odds are that at the end of that rather feeble explanation, your friends will say what filmmakers everywhere fear most: "What else is playing?"

All because you couldn't answer a simple question: "What is it?"

"What is it?" is the name of the game. "What is it?" *is* the movie. A good "What is it?" is the coin of the realm.

Let's CUT TO: Monday morning in Hollywood.

The results are in from the weekend. The burning wreckage of the big box-office disaster is smoking on the front page of *Variety*. The makers of the surprise hit that stunned everybody are still working the phones saying: "I knew it! I told you so!" And for everyone else the process is starting all over again:

> A producer and writer are in some movie executive's office about to pitch their "big idea."

> An agent is on the phone describing the script her client wrote that she read over the weekend and loves!

> An executive is meeting with the studio's marketing team trying to figure out what the poster should look like for their upcoming summer release.

Everyone, all across town, in a position to buy or in the effort to sell, is trying to wrap their brains around the same question your friends were asking on Saturday night: "What is it?"

And if they can't, they're toast.

If you think this sounds cold, if you can't believe that Hollywood doesn't care about "story" or the artistic vision of the filmmakers, trust me, it's only going to get worse. It's because just like you with your newspaper trying to pitch your friends their movie choices, the competition for our attention spans has gotten fierce.

There are movies, TV, radio, the Internet, and music. There are 300 channels of cable; there are magazines; and there are sports. In truth, on any given weekend, even an avid moviegoer only has about 30 seconds to decide what to see. And what about those moviegoers who aren't so avid? How are you going to cut through all the traffic that's competing for their attention and communicate with *them*?

There are just too many choices.

So the studios try to make it easy to choose. That's why they produce so many sequels and remakes. They call them "pre-sold franchises" — and get ready to see a lot more of them.

A **pre-sold franchise** is something that a goodly chunk of the audience is already "sold" on. It cuts way down on the "What is it?" factor because most people already kind of know. Some recent examples include *Starsky and Hutch*, *The Hulk*, and *Resident Evil*, based on a TV show, a comic book, and a video game respectively — and each with a built-in fan base. There's also a plague of sequels: *Shrek 2*, *Spider-Man 2*, *Mission: Impossible 3*, *Ocean's Twelve*. It's not that Hollywood is creatively bankrupt; the decision-makers just don't think that you out there with your newspapers every Saturday really, deep down, want to try anything new. Why gamble your 10 bucks on something you're not sure of versus something you already know?

And maybe they're right. If you can't answer "What is it?" why take a chance?

The problem for us, the spec screenwriters of the world, is that we don't own any of these pre-sold franchises nor are we likely to. We're the guys and gals with a laptop computer and a dream. How are *we* going to come up with something as good as *Lawrence of Arabia* that will sell like *Spy Kids 3-D*? Well, there is a way. But to try it, I want you to do something daring. I want you to forget all about your screenplay for now, the cool scenes that are bursting forth in your imagination, the soundtrack, and the stars you KNOW would be interested in being in it. Forget all that.

And concentrate on writing one sentence. One line.

Because if you can learn how to tell me "What is it?" better, faster, and with more creativity, you'll keep me interested. And incidentally, by doing so before you start writing your script, you'll make the story better, too.

THE LOGLINE FROM HELL

I talk to lots of screenwriters, I've been pitched by experts and amateurs, and my question when they prematurely drift into the story of their movie is always the same: "What's the one-line?" Oddly, this is often the last thing screenwriters think about when writing a script. Believe me, I've been there. You're so involved in your scenes, you're so jazzed about being able to tie in that symbolic motif from *The Odyssey*, you've got it all so mapped out, that you forget one simple thing: You can't tell me what it's about. You can't get to the heart of the story in less than 10 minutes.

Boy, are you screwed!

And I personally refuse to listen.

It's because I know the writer hasn't thought it through. Not really. Because a good screenwriter, especially anyone writing on spec, has to think about everyone all down the line, from the agent to the producer to the studio head to the public. You won't be there to "set the mood," so how are you going to get strangers excited? And getting *them* excited is Job One. So I cut writers off at their FADE IN: because I know everyone else will too. If you can't tell me about it in one quick line, well, buddy I'm on to something else. Until you have your pitch, and it grabs me, don't bother with the story.

In Hollywood parlance it's called a **logline** or a **one-line**. And the difference between a good one and a bad one is simple. When I pick up the trades and read the logline of a spec or a pitch that's sold and my first reaction is "Why didn't *I* think of that?!" Well… that's a good one. At random I'm going to select a few recent sales (from my Web source: *www.hollywoodlitsales.com*) that made me jealous. They're in my genre, family comedy, but what we can learn from them crosses comedy, drama, whatever. Each of these was a big, fat spec sale in the six-to-seven figure range:

> A newly married couple must spend Christmas Day at each of their four divorced parent's homes — *4 Christmases*

> A just-hired employee goes on a company weekend and soon discovers someone's trying to kill him — *The Retreat*

> A risk-averse teacher plans on marrying his dream girl but must first accompany his overprotective future brother-in-law — a cop — on a ride along from hell! — *Ride Along* (Please note: Anything "from hell" is always a comedy plus.)

Believe it or not, each of these loglines has the same things in common. Along with answering "What is it?" each contains four components that make it a sale.

What are those four components?

Well, let's investigate... *the logline from hell!*

ISN'T IT IRONIC?

The number one thing a good logline must have, the single most important element, is: irony. My good friend and former writing partner, the funny and fast-typing Colby Carr, pointed this out to me one time and he's 100% correct. And that goes for whether it's a comedy or a drama.

> A cop comes to L.A. to visit his estranged wife and her office building is taken over by terrorists — *Die Hard*

> A businessman falls in love with a hooker he hires to be his date for the weekend — *Pretty Woman*

I don't know about you, but I think both of these loglines, one from a drama, one from a romantic comedy, fairly reek of irony. And irony gets my attention. It's what we who struggle with loglines like to call **the hook**, because that's what it does. It *hooks* your interest.

What is intriguing about each of the spec sales I've cited above is that they, too, have that same ironic touch. A holiday season of supposed family joy is turned on its cynical head in the *4 Christmases* example. What could be more unexpected (another way to say "ironic") for a new employee, instead of being welcomed to a company, to be faced with a threat on his life during

The Retreat? What Colby identified is the fact that a good logline must be emotionally intriguing, like an itch you *have* to scratch.

A logline is like the cover of a book; a good one makes you want to open it, right now, to find out what's inside. In identifying the ironic elements of your story and putting them into a logline, you may discover that you don't have that. Well, if you don't, then there may not only be something wrong with your logline — maybe your story's off, too. And maybe it's time to go back and rethink it. Insisting on irony in your logline is a good place to find out what's missing. Maybe you don't have a good movie yet.

A COMPELLING MENTAL PICTURE

The second most important element that a good logline has is that you must be able to see a whole movie in it. Like Proust's *madeleine*, a good logline, once said, blossoms in your brain. You see the movie, or at least the potential for it, and the mental images it creates offer the promise of more. One of my personal favorites is producer David Permut's pitch for *Blind Date*: "She's the perfect woman — until she has a drink." I don't know about you, but I *see* it. I see a beautiful girl and a date gone bad and a guy who wants to save it because... she's the one! There's a lot going on in that one-line, far more than in the actual movie, but that's a different subject altogether. The point is that a good logline, in addition to pulling you in, has to offer the promise of more.

In the above examples for new spec script sales, we even see where each film begins and ends, don't we? Although I haven't read more than the one-line for *Ride Along*, I think this movie will probably take place in one night, like *After Hours*. That actually goes for each of those examples. All three loglines clearly demarcate a time frame in which their story takes place: Christmas Day, the weekend of a corporate retreat, and in the case of *Ride Along*, a single night.

In addition, the *Ride Along* example offers an obvious comic conflict as opposites face off over a common goal. It will take a naïve, scaredy-cat teacher and throw him into the crime-ridden world of his brother-in-law, the cop. This is why "fish-out-of-water" stories are so popular: You can see the potential fireworks of one type of person being thrust into a world outside his ken. In that one set-up line a whole story blooms with possibilities.

Does your logline offer this? Does giving me the set-up of your comedy or drama make my imagination run wild with where I think the story will go? If it doesn't, you haven't got the logline yet. And I'll say it again: *If you don't have the logline, maybe you should rethink your whole movie.*

AUDIENCE AND COST

Another thing a good logline has, that is important in attracting studio buyers, is a built-in sense of who it's for and what it's going to cost.

Let's take *4 Christmases* for example. I'll bet they're going after the same audience that *Meet The Parents* and its sequel *Meet the Fockers* found. Both of these are medium-cost, **four-quadrant pictures** that seek to attract the broadest possible audience. From the elements I see inherent in the *4 Christmases* pitch, it's what the writers are trying for. They're going to get two twenty-something stars to pull in the core target — young people — and they're going to stunt cast the parents' roles with stars the older crowd likes. Can we get Jack or Robin or Dustin? Well, sure! Look how well De Niro did in *Meet The Parents*!

I also know from the logline that the movie's not expensive. Sure there may be a car chase or two and a Christmas tree fire (I'm guessing) but basically it's a **block comedy** — so called because it takes place... on the block. There are few "company moves" where cast and crew have to travel. It's cheap. If I'm an executive who's looking for a general audience, medium budget (depending on the stars) Christmas perennial, this sounds just about perfect for my needs. I know what I'm dealing with in terms of audience and cost.

Send it over!

And someone obviously did.

That's a whole lot to ask from one lousy line of description, don't you think? But it's right there.

Does your logline contain that kind of information?

A KILLER TITLE

Lastly, what is intriguing about a good logline must include the title. Title and logline are, in fact, the one-two punch, and a good combo never fails to knock me out. Like the irony in a good logline, a great title must have irony *and* tell the tale. One of the best titles of recent memory, and one I still marvel at, is *Legally Blonde*. When I think about all the bad titles it could have been — *Barbie Goes To Harvard, Totally Law School, Airhead Apparent* — to come up with one that nails the concept, without being so **on the nose** that it's stupid, is an art unto itself. I am jealous of that title. A good sign!

My favorite bad title ever, just to give you an idea of what doesn't work for me, is *For Love or Money*. There've been four movies with that title that I know of, one starring Michael J. Fox, and I can't tell you the plot of any of them. You could probably call every movie ever made *For Love or Money* and be right — technically. It just shows how un-daring a generic title can be and how something vague like that kills your interest in paying $10 to see it.

One of the key ingredients in a good title, however, is that it *must* be the headline of the story. Again I cite *4 Christmases* as an example. While it's not a world-beater, it's not bad. But it does the one thing that a good title must do, and I'll highlight it because it's vital that you get this:

It says what it is!

They could have called *4 Christmases* something more vague, how about *Yuletide*? That says "Christmas," right? But it doesn't pin-point what this particular Christmas movie is about. It doesn't say what it is, which is a movie about one couple spending four different Christmases with four different sets of families on the same Christmas day. If it doesn't pass the Say What It Is Test, you don't have your title. And you don't have the one-two punch that makes a great logline.

I admit that often I have come up with the title first and made the story match. That's how I thought up a script I went on to co-write and sell called *Nuclear Family*. At first all I had was the title, then I came up with the ironic twist. Instead of nuclear as in "father, mother, and children" the way the term is meant, why not nuclear as in "radioactive." The logline became: "A dysfunctional family goes camping on a nuclear dumpsite and wakes up the next morning with super powers." With the help of my writing partner, the quick-witted and jet-setting Jim Haggin, we fleshed out that story and sold the script in a bidding war to Steven Spielberg for $1 million. Our title and logline met all the criteria cited above: irony, promise of more, audience and cost (four-quadrant, with special effects, not stars), and one that definitely said what it is.

It's a movie I *still* want to see, if anyone's listening.

YOU AND YOUR "WHAT IS IT?"

All good screenwriters are bullheads.

There, I said it.

But I mean it in a *nice* way! Because if there's anyone who understands the occasional arrogance of the screenwriter, it's *moi*. To be a screenwriter is to deal with an ongoing tug of war between breathtaking megalomania and insecurity so deep it takes years of therapy just to be able to say "I'm a writer" out loud. This is especially so among the spec screenwriting crowd I like to hang with. We come up with our movie ideas, we start to "create," we SEE it so clearly, that often by the time we're writing that sucker, it's too late to turn back. We're going to bullhead our way through this script no matter what anyone says. But I am suggesting that you say "whoa" to all that. I'm proposing that before you head off into your FADE IN: you think long and hard about the logline, the title, and the poster.

And even do some test marketing.

What's that, you ask?

A TEST MARKETING EXAMPLE

I have posed the possibility that you hold off on writing your script until you get a killer logline and title. I know this is painful. But here's where it pays off. I have just been working with a screenwriter online. He did not have his logline. He *did* have a good idea — or at least the start of one — but the logline was vague, it didn't grab me. I sent him back to the dreaded **Page One** (an almost total rewrite). He bitched and moaned, but he did it.

He put away his story and all the vivid scenes and the recurring motifs and started writing loglines — an awful, soul-eating chore. He tried to come up with ones that were still his story, but which met the criteria. What he discovered, after many failed attempts, was that he had to start fudging his logline to get it to have irony, audience and cost, a clear sense of what the movie promised, and a killer title. And when he finally let go of his preconceived notions of what his story was — voila! The logline changed.

Soon, he started getting better response from people he pitched to, and suddenly, voila! #2 — his story started to change to match the logline, and voila! #3 — the story got better! The irony of what he *sort of* had was brought into better focus. And when it was put into a pithy logline form, the conflicts were brought into sharper focus too. They had to! Or else the logline wouldn't work. The characters became more distinct, the story became more clearly defined, and the logline ultimately made the actual writing easier.

The best thing about what this screenwriter discovered is that he saved everybody, all down the line, a whole lot of money and trouble. Can you imagine trying to do these kinds of logline fixes during postproduction? It's a little late by then. Before anyone spent a dime, using only paper, pencil, and his own wits, he did everyone's job for them. He not only made it easier for the guy with the newspaper to pitch to his friends, but he gave them a better story once they got to the movie theater. All because he had given his project a better "What is it?"

The other great part about road-testing your logline is that you have the experience of all-weather pitching. I pitch to anyone who will stand still. I do it in line at Starbucks. I do it with friends and strangers. I always spill my guts when it comes to discussing what I'm working on, because:

a. I have no fear that anyone will steal my idea (and anyone who has that fear is an amateur) and...

b. You find out more about your movie by talking to people one-on-one than having them read it.

This is what I mean by "test marketing."

When I am about to go pitch a studio, when I am working on a new idea for a movie, or when I can't decide which of four or five ideas is best, I talk to "civilians." I talk to them and I look in their eyes as I'm talking. When they start to drift, when they look away, I've lost them. And I know my pitch has problems. So I make sure that when I pitch to my next victim, I've corrected whatever slow spot or confusing element I overlooked the first time out. And most of all, it's really fun to do.

A typical scenario goes like this:

INT. COFFEE BEAN AND TEA LEAF — SUNSET PLAZA — DAY
A mélange of starlets, weekend Hell's Angels, and Eurotrash snobs sip double mocha frappes. Blake Snyder eyes the crowd. He approaches the person who seems least likely to hit him.

                    BLAKE SNYDER
          Hi, could you help me?

                    STRANGER
               (dubious)
          What is it? I have a Pilates class
          in ten minutes.

                    BLAKE SNYDER
          Perfect, this will only take a
          second. I'm working on a movie idea
          and I wanted to know what you think.

```
                        STRANGER
                (smiling, looks at watch)
        Okay...
```

This, to me, is the perfect set-up and one that I repeat with all age groups, in all kinds of situations, all over Southern California — but especially with the target audience of whatever I'm working on.

This kind of test marketing is not only a great way to meet people, it's the only way to know what you've got. And a "pitchee" who is thinking about being somewhere else is the perfect subject. If you can get *his* attention, if you can *keep* his attention, and if he wants to know more about the story you're telling, you've really got a good movie idea.

What you'll also find by getting out from behind your computer and talking to people is how that true-life experience that happened to you in summer camp in 1972, the story that you are basing your entire screenplay on that means so much to you, means nothing to a stranger. To get and keep that stranger's attention, you're going to have to figure out a way to present a compelling "What is it?" that does mean something to him. Or you're going to be wasting your time. There are a lot more strangers than friends buying tickets to movies. No matter who is encouraging you on the friend side of your life, it's the strangers you really need to impress.

What better way to find out what you've got than to actually go out and ask?

THE "DEATH" OF HIGH CONCEPT

All of the above dances around a term that many people in Hollywood hate: **high concept**. The term was made famous by Jeffrey Katzenberg and Michael Eisner in their heyday as young gurus running Disney.

To them it meant just what we've been discussing here — making the movie easier to see — and they came up with a long run of successful high concept movies. All you had to do was look at the **one-sheet** (another name for the poster) and you knew "What is it?" for *Ruthless People*, *Outrageous Fortune*, and *Down and Out in Beverly Hills*. Like most fashionable terms it's now out to say your project is high concept. The death of high concept has been proclaimed many times. But like a lot of what I'm going to discuss throughout this book, I care less about what is *au currant* and more about what works and what is simple common sense.

In my opinion, thinking "high concept," thinking about "What is it?" is just good manners, common courtesy if you will. It's a way to put yourself in the shoes of the customer, the person who's paying good money, including parking and a babysitter, to come and see your film. And don't kid yourself, as brilliant as these two visionaries are, Michael Eisner and Jeffrey Katzenberg didn't invent high concept, it's been around from the beginning.

Think about every Preston Sturges movie hit from the 1940s — *Christmas In July*, *Hail the Conquering Hero*, *Lady Eve*, even *Sullivan's Travels* — all high concept ideas that drew people into theatres based on the logline and poster.

Think about every Alfred Hitchcock thriller ever made — *Rear Window*, *North by Northwest*, *Vertigo* and *Psycho*.

Just mentioning these movies to a true fan evokes the pitch and the poster of each story. And check out those titles. All of them, across the board, certainly say what it is and they do so in a way that's not on the nose or stupid (well, *Psycho* is potentially lame, but we'll let him off the hook on that one — it's Hitchcock, after all).

The point is that if someone gives you static about your high concept idea, just smile and know that clearly and creatively presenting a better "What is it?" to a potential audience — no matter who they are or what position they occupy in the chain — never goes out of fashion. I defy those who think this is a game for salesmen and not filmmakers to come up with a better title than *Legally Blonde*. And as we will see in the next chapter, we're only at the beginning of finding ways to put yourself in the shoes of the moviegoer.

And that is what we should *all* be doing more of.

SUMMARY

So are your synapses starting to misfire? Are the growing pains too much? Well, whether this is old news or new news, the "What is it?" is the only place to begin this task of ours. The job of the screenwriter, especially one writing on spec, must include consideration for everyone all along the way, from agent to producer to the studio exec who decides what gets made. And that job starts with that question: "What is it?"

Along with a good "What is it?" a movie must have a clear sense of what it's about and who it's for. Its tone, potential, the dilemma of its characters, and the type of characters they are, should be easy to understand and compelling.

In order to better create a good "What is it?" the spec screenwriter must be able to tell a good one-line or logline — a one- or two-sentence grabber that tells us everything. It must satisfy four basic elements to be effective:

 1. Irony. It must be in some way ironic and emotionally involving — a dramatic situation that is like an itch you have to scratch.

2. A compelling mental picture. It must bloom in your mind when you hear it. A whole movie must be implied, often including a time frame.

3. Audience and cost. It must demarcate the tone, the target audience, and the sense of cost, so buyers will know if it can make a profit.

4. A killer title. The one-two punch of a good logline must include a great title, one that "says what it is" and does so in a clever way.

This is all part of what is called "high concept," a term that came about to describe movies that are easy to see. In fact, high concept is more important than ever before, especially since movies must be sold internationally, too. Domestic box office used to account for 60% of a movie's overall profit, but that figure is down to 40%. That means movies must travel and be understood *everywhere* — over half of your market is now outside the U.S. So while high concept is a term that's not fashionable, it's a type of movie all Hollywood is actively looking for. You just have to figure out a quicker, slicker way to provide high concept ideas.

Finally, this is all about intriguing the audience, so a good way to road test an idea is to get out from behind your computer and pitch it. Pitch your movie to anyone who will listen and adjust accordingly. You never know what valuable information you can learn from a stranger with a blank expression.

EXERCISES

1. Pick up the newspaper and pitch this week's movie choices to a friend. Can you think of ways to improve the movie's logline or poster?

2. If you are already working on a screenplay, or if you have several in your files, write the loglines for each and present them to a stranger. By pitching in this way, do you find the logline changing? Does it make you think of things you should have tried in your script? Does the story have to change to fit the pitch?

3. Grab a *TV Guide* and read the loglines from the movie section. Does the logline and title of a movie say what it is? Do vague loglines equate with a movie's failure in your mind? Was its lack of a good "What is it?" responsible in any way for that failure?

4. If you don't have an idea for a screenplay yet, try these five games to jump-start your movie idea skills:

   a. GAME #1a: Funny _____
   Pick a drama, thriller, or horror film and turn it into a comedy. Example: Funny *Christine* — The haunted dream car of a teenage boy that ruins his life now becomes a comedy when the car starts giving dating advice.

   b. GAME #1b: Serious _____
   Likewise, pick a comedy and make it into a drama. Serious *Animal House* — Drama about cheating scandal at a small university ends in *A Few Good Men*-like showdown.

c. GAME #2: FBI out of water

This works for comedy or drama. Name five places that a
FBI agent in the movies has never been sent to solve a
crime. Example: "Stop or I'll Baste!": Slob FBI agent is
sent undercover to a Provence Cooking School.

d. GAME #3: _____ School

Works for both drama and comedy. Name five examples
of an unusual type of school, camp, or classroom.
Example: "Wife School": Women sent by their rich husbands soon rebel.

e. GAME #4: VERSUS!!!

Drama or comedy. Name several pairs of people to be on
opposite sides of a burning issue. Example: A hooker and
a preacher fall in love when a new massage parlor divides
the residents of a small town.

f. GAME #5: My_____ Is A Serial Killer

Drama or comedy. Name an unusual person, animal, or
thing that a paranoid can suspect of being a murderer.
Example: "My Boss Is A Serial Killer." Guy gets promoted
every time a dead body turns up at the corporation — is the
murderer his employer?

And if you come up with a really good logline for a family comedy,
here is my e-mail address: *bsnyder264@aol.com*. I'd be happy to
hear a good one... if you think you've got it.

2 GIVE ME THE SAME THING... ONLY DIFFERENT!

A screenwriter's daily conundrum is how to avoid cliché.

You can be near the cliché, you can dance around it, you can run right up to it and *almost* embrace it.

But at the last second you must turn away.

You must give it a twist.

And insisting on those twists, defying that inner voice that says "Oh, well, no one will notice," is a universal struggle that good storytellers have been fighting forever.

To quote the studio executive who first blurted out this rule to me, Sam Goldwyn-like, during a development meeting: "Give me the same thing... only different!"

Bless his pointy little head.

In every aspect of creation — from the idea, to the way characters speak, to the scenes themselves — putting a fresh spin on it (whatever "it" is) is what we do every day. But to know how to avoid the cliché, to know what tradition you are pushing forward, begins with knowing what that tradition is. A full-fledged knowledge of hundreds of movies, and especially those which your movie is like, is required.

Yet surprising as it seems for people who are interested in pursuing a career in movies, I am shocked — *shocked!* — to find how many up-and-comers can not even quote from movies in their own genre, much less movies generally.

Trust me, all the big guys can.

Listen to Spielberg or Scorsese talk about movies. They know and can quote from hundreds. And I don't mean quote as in "recite lines from," I mean quote as in "explain how each movie works." Movies are intricately made emotion machines. They are Swiss watches of precise gears and spinning wheels that make them tick. You have to be able to take them apart and put them back together again. In the dark. In your sleep. And your knowledge of a few movies you like is not enough. It is also not enough to know all the movies of the past five years. You have to go back, see the lineage of many types of movies, know what movie begat what in the line of succession, and how the art was advanced by each.

Which leads me to the subject of *genre*.

You are about to embark on the next step of writing a successful screenplay and that is the categorizing of your movie idea. *But no!* you think. *My movie is new! It's like nothing ever seen before! I will not be put into a category!*

Sorry. Too late.

You can't tell me any idea that isn't like one, or dozens, found in the movie canon. Trust me, your movie falls into a category. And that category has rules that you need to know. Because to explode the clichés, to give us the same thing... only different, you have to know what genre your movie is part of, and how to invent the twists that avoid pat elements. If you can do that, you have a better chance to sell. And, by the way, everyone, and I mean *everyone* in Hollywood, already does this. So why not know what they know?

WHAT IS IT... MOST LIKE?

So now you've got your logline.

You've followed my advice, you've gone out and test pitched your dozen or so "victims," you've got their responses and adjusted accordingly, and now your one-liner is just shining there so brightly! You know you've got yourself a winner.

You're ready to type FADE IN: — right?

Wrong.

I'm holding you back because before you start writing I want you to think a little bit about the question after "What is it?" — and that's "What is it... *most like?*"

I return again to the example of you and your friends on Saturday night. You've pitched them their movie choices, and they've picked a couple. And now they want to know more about what they can expect to see when they plunk down their $10. Okay, so it's a comedy. But what kind?

This situation is why you hear so many bad movie pitches in Hollywood. They're the ones, I admit, that I've used as shorthand, but which I really hate and don't advise you to use. These are the types of pitches people make fun of — and rightly so. "It's *X-Men* meets *Cannonball Run!*" the nervous pitcher will say. Or "*It's Die Hard* in a bowling alley!" The ones that combine two or more movies are especially irksome. You sit there, trying to imagine how "It's *Heathers* meets *M*A*S*H*" really works. What is that? Spoiled teenage girls join the Army? A medical team is airlifted to a high school to save kids who are shooting each other? What? And odds are all the pitcher is doing is grabbing two hit movies and hoping there's some element in there that someone will like.

(PLEASE NOTE: You never use bombs to describe these mad doctor experiments; it's never "*Ishtar* meets *Howard the Duck*" — an example which tells you exactly how bad a technique this is.)

And yet... I admit I do it.

The reason categorizing your movie is a good idea is that it's important for you, the screenwriter, to know what type of movie you're writing. Of the many ways to get lost while in the middle of writing a screenplay, this is the most common. When I am writing a movie, when *Steven Spielberg* is writing a movie, referencing other movies, looking for clues of plotting and character within the genre, is commonplace. And thus, when you are stuck in your story or when you're preparing to write, you will "screen" a dozen movies that are like the one you're working on to get clues about why certain plot elements are important, why they work or don't, and where you can change the cliché into something fresh.

There are 10 movie genres that have proven to be good places to start this process. That's all they are, a place to start — we'll get into how to move past them next.

As I search for matches in this game of genre gin rummy — do I look for runs or pairs? — I'm interested in creating categories of movies that I can add more movies to every year. And I think within these 10 story types, you can stick just about every motion picture ever made. You can make up your own categories, you can add others to this list, but I hope you won't need to. You will also note that nowhere in this list do I have standard genre types, such as Romantic Comedy, Epic, or Biography — because those names don't really tell me anything about what the story is. And that's what I need to know.

The 10 types of movies I have categorized here are:

Monster in the House — Of which *Jaws, Tremors, Alien, The Exorcist, Fatal Attraction*, and *Panic Room* are examples.

Golden Fleece — This is the category of movie best exemplified by *Star Wars; The Wizard of Oz; Planes, Trains and Automobiles; Back To The Future;* and most "heist movies."

Out of the Bottle — This incorporates films like *Liar, Liar; Bruce Almighty; Love Potion #9; Freaky Friday; Flubber;* and even my own little kid hit from Disney, *Blank Check.*

Dude with a Problem — This is a genre that ranges in style, tone, and emotional substance from *Breakdown* and *Die Hard* to *Titanic* and *Schindler's List.*

Rites Of Passage — Every change-of-life story from *10* to *Ordinary People* to *Days of Wine and Roses* makes this category.

Buddy Love — This genre is about more than the buddy movie dynamic as seen in cop buddy pictures, *Dumb & Dumber*, and *Rain Man* — but also every love story ever made!

Whydunit — Who cares *who*, it's *why* that counts. Includes *Chinatown, China Syndrome, JFK*, and *The Insider.*

The Fool Triumphant — One of the oldest story types, this category includes *Being There*, *Forrest Gump*, *Dave*, *The Jerk*, *Amadeus*, and the work of silent clowns like Chaplin, Keaton, and Lloyd.

Institutionalized — Just like it sounds, this is about groups: *Animal House*, *M*A*S*H*, *One Flew Over the Cuckoo's Nest*, and "family" sagas such as *American Beauty* and *The Godfather*.

Superhero — This isn't just about the obvious tales you'd think of, like *Superman* and *Batman*, but also includes *Dracula*, *Frankenstein*, even *Gladiator* and *A Beautiful Mind*.

Are you thoroughly confused? Do you doubt my sanity when I tell you that *Schindler's List* and *Die Hard* are in the same category? Are you looking at me kinda funny when I tell you that buddy movies are just love stories in disguise? Good! Then let's dig further into the wonderful world of genre.

MONSTER IN THE HOUSE

What do *Jaws*, *The Exorcist*, and *Alien* have in common? They're examples of the genre I call "Monster in the House." This genre has a long track record and was probably the first tale Man ever told. It has two working parts: A monster. A house. And when you add people into that house, desperate to kill the monster, you've got a movie type so primal that it translates to everyone, everywhere. It's the type of movie that I like to say, "You can pitch to a caveman." It's not about being dumb, it's about being **primal**. And *everyone* understands the simple, primal commandment: Don't... Get... Eaten!

That's why this genre is responsible for so many worldwide hits and franchises. You can probably run most of these films without the soundtrack and still "get it." *Jurassic Park*; the *Nightmare On Elm*

Street, *Friday the 13th*, and *Scream* series; *Tremors* and its sequels; and every haunted house and ghost story ever told are all examples of this genre. Even films without supernatural elements, like *Fatal Attraction* (starring Glenn Close as the "Monster"), fall into this category. And it's clear from such movies as *Arachnophobia*, *Lake Placid*, and *Deep Blue Sea*, if you don't know the rules of Monster in the House — you fail.

The rules, to me, are simple. The "house" must be a confined space: a beach town, a spaceship, a futuristic Disneyland with dinosaurs, a family unit. There must be sin committed — usually greed (monetary or carnal) — prompting the creation of a supernatural monster that comes like an avenging angel to kill those who have committed that sin and spare those who realize what that sin is. The rest is "run and hide." And putting a new twist on both the monster, the monster's powers, and the way we say "Boo!" is the job of the screenwriter who wants to add to the illustrious limb of this family tree of movies.

We can see a bad example of this category in *Arachnophobia*, the film starring Jeff Daniels and John Goodman. Bad monster: a little spider. Not much supernatural there. Not all that scary either — you step on it and it dies. Also: No house! At any given moment, the residents of *Arachnophobia* can say "Check please" and be on the next Greyhound out of town.

Where is the tension there?

Because the filmmakers behind *Arachnophobia* violated the rules of Monster in the House, they wound up with a mishmash. Is it a comedy or a drama? Are we really supposed to be *scared*-scared? I could write a whole book on the rules of Monster in the House, but you don't need me to have a MITH film festival in your own home and discover these nuances for yourself. And if you're writing a screenplay that falls into this genre, I suggest you do just that.

I want to make clear that, as with all the genres to be discussed here, this is a category that has not, repeat *not*, been exhausted. There is always a way to do a new one. But you must give it a fresh twist to be successful. You must break from cliché. You must "Give us the same thing... only different." Anyone who thinks there isn't new territory to mine in the Monster in the House genre, should think of the myth of the Minotaur. Great Monster: a half-man/half-bull. Great house: a maze where the condemned are sent to die. But the ancient Greek hack who eyed this successful story and said: "It's over. Genre's dead. I can't top that!" never envisioned Glenn Close with a bad perm and a boiled rabbit.

THE GOLDEN FLEECE

The quest myth has been one of the more winning tales told around the campfire since, well, forever. And if your screenplay can in any way be categorized as a "Road Movie," then you must know the rules of a genre I call "The Golden Fleece." The name comes from the myth of Jason and the Argonauts and yet it's always about the same thing: A hero goes "on the road" in search of one thing and winds up discovering something else — himself. Thus *Wizard Of Oz*; *Planes, Train and Automobiles*; *Star Wars*; *Road Trip*; and *Back to the Future* are all basically the same movie.

Scary, huh?

Like the twists of any story, the milestones of The Golden Fleece are the people and incidents that our hero or heroes encounter along the way. Because it's episodic it seems to not be connected, but it must be. The theme of every Golden Fleece movie is internal growth; how the incidents affect the hero is, in fact, the plot. It is the way we know that we are truly making forward progress — it's not the mileage we're racking up that makes a good Golden Fleece, it's the way the hero changes as he goes. And forcing those milestones to mean something to the hero is your job.

As it turns out, I have been working on a Golden Fleece with my current writing partner, the amazingly successful and talented Sheldon Bull. And we have been discussing Golden Fleece movies a lot — naturally. Since our film is a comedy, we've looked at *Planes, Trains and Automobiles*, and discussed the character dynamics of *Rain Man*, *Road Trip*, and even *Animal House*, believe it or not, in an effort to get a handle on what is basically the story of a kid who heads home after being unjustly kicked out of military school and discovers... *that his parents have moved without telling him!* It's basically "*Home Alone* on the road." (Sorry! It's a bad habit). The adjustments we are making aren't about the adventure — which I find hilarious — but about what each incident means to our kid hero. In many ways what these adventures are is irrelevant. Whatever fun **set pieces** our hero encounters must be shaded to deliver milestones of growth for our kid lead. We always come back to that Golden Fleece truism that can be found in *The Odyssey*, *Gulliver's Travels*, and any number of successful road stories through the ages: It's not the incidents, it's what the hero learns about himself from those incidents that makes the story work.

This genre is also where all heist movies are found. Any quest, mission, or "treasure locked in a castle" that is to be approached by an individual or a group falls into the Golden Fleece category and has the same rules. Very often the mission becomes secondary to other, more personal, discoveries; the twists and turns of the plot are suddenly less important than the meaning derived from the heist, as *Ocean's Eleven*, *The Dirty Dozen*, and *The Magnificent Seven* prove.

OUT OF THE BOTTLE

"I wish I had my own money!" This is what our character Preston Waters states in the movie *Colby Carr* and I wrote and sold to Disney that became a kid's mini-hit called *Blank Check*. And

Preston will, in fact, soon get his own money — a million dollars to be exact — with which he will happily run amok. This type of wish-fulfillment is so common because it's a big part of the human psyche. "I wish I had a_____" is probably the single most frequently spoken prayer since Adam. And stories that tell a good "what if" tale that exploits these wish fulfillment fantasies are good, primal, easy-for-a-caveman-to-understand stories — which is why they're so many of them. And why they're so successful.

The comedy hit *Bruce Almighty* is an example of this genre. In fact, the flexible Jim Carrey has also been the star of another "Out of the Bottle" classic, *The Mask*. It doesn't have to be God who bestows the magic. It can be a thing — like *The Mask* or a magic VW named "Herbie" in Disney's *The Love Bug*, or a formula that you invent to make the opposite sex fall in love with you as in *Love Potion #9* starring Sandra Bullock, or magic silly-putty that can save your teaching career as in *Flubber* starring Robin Williams.

The name Out of the Bottle should evoke the image of a genie who is summoned out of the bottle to grant his master's wish, but it doesn't have to be magic to be part of this wish-fulfillment genre. In *Blank Check*, there is no magic that gets Preston his million bucks — sure it's a long shot, and Colby and I went out of our way to make it seem reality-based. But it doesn't matter. Whether it's by divine intervention or luck or a magic being who enters the scene, it's the same device. For some reason or other, usually because we like the guy or gal and think they deserve it, their wish is granted and their lives begin to change.

On the flip side of Out of the Bottle, but very much the same category, is the curse aspect of wishing. These are comeuppance tales. Another Jim Carrey movie, *Liar, Liar*, is a good example (hmmm, are we seeing a pattern here about what stars consistently fit best into what Jungian archetypes?). Same set-up, same device — a kid wishes his lying lawyer father would start telling nothing but the truth — and lo! It happens. Suddenly Jim Carrey can't tell a lie — on the day of a big case in which lying is, and has been, his best weapon. Jim's going to have to change his ways and grow if he is to survive, and by doing so, he gets what he really wants in the first place: the respect of his wife and son. Another comeuppance tale is *Freaky Friday*, both the Jodie Foster version and the updated Lindsay Lohan take. But there are many of these, such as *All Of Me* with Steve Martin and *Groundhog Day* starring another famous wise guy, Bill Murray.

The rules of Out of the Bottle then are this: If it's a wish-fulfillment tale, the hero must be a put-upon Cinderella who is so under the thumb of those around him that we are really rooting for anyone, or anything, to get him a little happiness. And yet, so the rules tell us and human nature dictates, we don't want to see anyone, even the most underdog character, succeed for too long. And eventually, the hero must learn that magic isn't everything, it's better to be just like us — us members of the audience — because in the end we know this will never happen to us. Thus a lesson must be in the offing; a good moral must be included at the end.

If it's a comeuppance tale version of Out of the Bottle, then the opposite set-up is applied. Here's a guy or gal who needs a swift kick in the behind. And yet, there must be something redeemable about them. This is a little trickier to pull off and must include a Save the Cat scene at the outset, one where we know that even though this guy or gal is a jerk, there is something in them that's worth saving. So in the course of the tale, they get the benefit of the magic (even though it's a curse); and in the end, they triumph.

DUDE WITH A PROBLEM
This genre is defined by the phrase: "An ordinary guy finds himself in extraordinary circumstances." And when you think about it,

it's another of the most popular, most primal situations we can imagine for ourselves. All of us consider ourselves to be an ordinary guy or gal, and thus we are drawn into sympathetic alignment with the hero of this type of tale from the get-go. Into this "just an ordinary day" beginning comes something extraordinary — my wife's building is taken over by terrorists with ponytails (*Die Hard*); Nazis start hauling away my Jewish friends (*Schindler's List*); a robot from the future (with an accent!) comes and tells me he is here to kill me and my unborn child (*The Terminator*); the ship in which we are traveling hits an iceberg and begins to sink without enough lifeboats for everyone on board (*Titanic*).

These, my friends, are problems. Big, *primal* problems.

So how are you, the ordinary guy, going to handle them?

Like Monster in the House, this genre also has two very simple working parts: a dude, meaning an average guy or gal just like ourselves. And a problem: something that this average guy must dig deep inside himself to conquer. From these simple components, an infinite number of mix-and-match situations can bloom and grow. The more average the guy, the bigger the challenge, as movies like *Breakdown* with Kurt Russell demonstrate.

In *Breakdown*, Kurt has no super powers or skills, no police training. Nada. But he shares with *Die Hard's* Bruce Willis the same domestic agenda all average guys understand: Save the wife that he loves! Whether our hero is skilled or not, it's the relative size of the challenge that makes these stories work. And one rule of thumb is: The badder the bad guy, the greater the heroics. So make the bad guy as bad as possible — always! — for the bigger the problem, the greater the odds for our dude to overcome. And no matter who the bad guy is, the dude triumphs from his willingness to use his individuality to outsmart the far more powerful forces aligned against him.

RITES OF PASSAGE

Remember the time you were awkwardly going through puberty and that cute girl you had a crush on didn't know you were alive? Remember that birthday party when you turned 40 and your husband came to you and asked for a divorce? These painful examples of life transition resonate with us because we have all, to a greater or lesser degree, gone through them. And growing-pain stories register because they are the most sensitive times in our lives. It's what makes us human, and what makes for excellent, poignant, and even hilarious storytelling. (Isn't Dudley Moore in *10* the funniest mid-life crisis put on film?) But whether it's drama or comedy, "Rites of Passage" tales are of a type. And all have the same rules.

All movies are about change, so to say that Rites of Passage stories document a change is missing the point. These are tales of pain and torment, but usually from an outside force: Life. Sure it's about the choices we've made, but the "monster" attacking us is often unseen, vague, or one which we can't get a handle on simply because we can't name it. *Lost Weekend*, *Days of Wine and Roses*, *28 Days* starring Sandra Bullock, and *When A Man Loves A Woman* starring Meg Ryan all tell stories about coming to grips with drugs and alcohol. Likewise, puberty, mid-life crisis, old age, romantic break-up, and "grieving" stories, like those about getting over the death of a loved one, such as *Ordinary People*, also have the same thing in common: In a good Rites of Passage tale, everybody's in on "the joke" except the person who's going through it — the story's hero. And only the experience can offer a solution.

In essence, whether the take is comedic or dramatic, the monster sneaks up on the beleaguered hero and the story is that hero's slow realization of who and what that monster is. In the end, these tales are about surrendering, the victory won by giving up to forces stronger than ourselves. The end point is acceptance of our humanity and the moral of the story is always the same: *That's Life!* (another Blake Edwards movie! Hmmm, between that, *10*, and *Days of Wine and Roses*, Blake Edwards appears to like and do well in this genre.)

If your movie idea can in any way be considered a Rites of Passage tale, then these films are fair game for screening. Like the steps of acceptance outlined in Elizabeth Kübler-Ross's *On Death and Dying*, the structure of this story type is charted in the hero's grudging acceptance of the forces of nature that he cannot control or comprehend, and the victory comes with the hero's ability to ultimately smile.

BUDDY LOVE

The classic "buddy story" is a type that I think of as a creation of the Movie Age. Though there were a few great buddy tales (*Don Quixote*, for example), this category really didn't take off as a story form until the dawn of cinema. My theory is that the buddy movie was invented by a screenwriter who realized that his hero had no one to react *to*. There was just this big, empty space where interior monologue and description is found in fiction. And the screenwriter suddenly thought "what if" his hero had someone to debate important story issues *with*? Thus the classic "buddy movie" was born, and from Laurel and Hardy to Bob Hope and Bing Crosby to *Butch Cassidy and the Sundance Kid* to the antics of *Wayne's World* (both 1 & 2), it has become a movie staple. Two guys talking to each other like *48 Hours*; two girls talking to each other like *Thelma & Louise*; two fish talking to each other like *Finding Nemo* — they all work because stories of "me and my best friend" will always resonate. Again, they're very human and based on universal circumstances. These are stories you can pitch to a caveman and both he (*and* his buddy!) will get it.

The secret of a good buddy movie is that it is actually a love story in disguise. And, likewise, all love stories are just buddy movies with the potential for sex. *Bringing Up Baby, Pat and Mike, Woman of the Year, Two Weeks Notice, How to Lose a Guy in 10 Days* are — genre-wise — just sophisticated *Laurel and Hardy* movies where one of the buddies is wearing a skirt. And yet the rules for these, drama or comedy, sex or no sex, are the same. At first the "buddies" hate each other. (Where would they have to go if they didn't?) But their adventure together brings out the fact that they need each other; they are, in essence, incomplete halves of a whole. And realizing this leads to even more conflict. Who can tolerate *needing* anybody?

Penultimately, the All Is Lost moment (more on this in Chapter Four) which occurs toward the end of each of these stories is: separation, a fight, a goodbye-and-good-riddance! that is, in reality, none of these. It's just two people who can't stand the fact that they don't live as well without each other, who will have to surrender their egos to win. And when the final curtain comes down, they have done just that.

Often, as in *Rain Man*, one of the buddies is the story's hero and will do all or most of the changing (i.e., Tom Cruise) while the other buddy acts as a catalyst of that change and will do slight or no changing (i.e., Dustin Hoffman). I have been in many story discussions about this dynamic. *Whose story is it??* is what it very often boils down to. *Lethal Weapon* is like that to an extent. It's Danny Glover's story. Mel Gibson is the agent of change. And though Mel will not be suicidal by the story's end, it's Danny Glover whose transformation we care most about. These "catalyst" Buddy Love tales, in which a "being" comes into one's life, affects it, and leaves, is a subset of the Buddy Love dynamic and an important one to keep in mind. Many "boy and his dog" tales are like this, including *E.T.*

If you're writing a buddy movie or love story, either drama or comedy, the dynamics of the Buddy Love structure are a must to know. Sit down with a dozen of these, pop 'em into your DVD player, and get ready to be amazed by how similar they all are. Is this stealing? Is Sandra Bullock ripping off Katherine Hepburn? Should Cary Grant's estate sue Hugh Grant for copyright infringement? Of course not. It's just good storytelling. And the beats are the same for a reason.

Because they always work.

WHYDUNIT

We all know that evil lurks in the hearts of men. Greed happens. Murder happens. And unseen evildoers are responsible for it all. But the "who" is never as interesting as the "why." Unlike the Golden Fleece, a good Whydunit isn't about the hero changing, it's about the audience discovering something about human nature they did not think was possible before the "crime" was committed and the "case" began. Like *Citizen Kane*, a classic Whydunit, the story is about seeking the innermost chamber of the human heart and discovering something unexpected, something dark and often unattractive, and the answer to the question: Why?

Chinatown is perhaps the best Whydunit ever made, and a textbook example of great screenwriting. It's one of those movies that you can see a thousand times and drive deeper into smaller and smaller rooms of the Nautilus shell with each viewing. What makes it a great Whydunit is what makes all classic Whydunits work. From *China Syndrome* to *All the President's Men* to *JFK* to *Mystic River*, every detective story or social drama, these stories walk on the dark side. They take us to the shadowy part of the street. And the rules are simple. We in the audience are the detectives, ultimately. While we have a surrogate or surrogates onscreen doing the work for us, it's we who must ultimately sift through the information, and we who must be shocked by what we find.

If your movie is about this type of discovery, take a look at the great Whydunits. Note how a surrogate onscreen represents us. And see why the investigation into the dark side of humanity is often an investigation into ourselves in an M.C. Escher-kaleidoscopic-reptile-eating-its-own-tail kinda way. That's what a good Whydunit does — it turns the x-ray machine back on ourselves and asks: "Are *we* this evil?"

THE FOOL TRIUMPHANT

The "Fool" is an important character in myth and legend and has been forever. On the outside, he's just the Village Idiot, but further examination reveals him to be the wisest among us. Being such an underdog gives the Fool the advantage of anonymity, and also makes everyone underestimate his ability, allowing him or her the chance to ultimately shine.

The Fool in the movies goes back to Chaplin, Keaton, and Lloyd. Little men, silly men, overlooked men, who triumph by luck and pluck and the specialness that comes from not giving up despite the odds. In modern movies, *Dave*, *Being There*, *Amadeus*, *Forrest Gump*, and many of the movies of Steve Martin, Bill Murray, and Ben Stiller come to mind as examples of how this tradition has evolved and why it will always have a place.

The operating principal of "The Fool Triumphant" is to set the underdog Fool against a bigger, more powerful, and often "establishment" bad guy. Watching a so-called "idiot" get the goat of those society deems to be the winners in life gives us all hope, and pokes fun at the structures we take so seriously in our day-to-day lives. Thus, no establishment is too sacred to be skewered, from the White House (*Dave*) to success in the business world (*The Jerk*) to the overblown reverence for the importance of our culture (*Forrest Gump*).

The working parts of a Fool Triumphant movie are simple: an underdog — who is seemingly so inept and so unequipped for life that everyone around him discounts his odds for success (and does so repeatedly in the set-up) — and an institution for that underdog to attack. Often, the Fool has an accomplice, an "insider" who is in on the joke and can't believe the Fool is getting away with his "ruse": Salieri in *Amadeus*, the Doctor in *Being There*, Lieutenant Dan in *Forrest Gump*. These characters often get the brunt of the slapstick, the guy at the end of the Rube Goldberg chain of events the Fool sets into motion, who ultimately gets the pie in the face, like Herbert Lom in *The Pink Panther*. Their crime is being close to the idiot, seeing him for what he really is, and being stupid enough to try to interfere.

Special Fools, whether they're in comedies or dramas like *Charly* and *Awakenings*, offer us a glimpse of the life of the outsider. We all feel like that at times, and tales of the Fool Triumphant give us the vicarious thrill of victory.

INSTITUTIONALIZED

Where would we be without each other? And when we band together as a group with a common cause, we reveal the ups and downs of sacrificing the goals of the few for those of the many. Thus, the genre I call "Institutionalized" tells stories about groups, institutions, and "families." These stories are special because they both honor the institution and expose the problems of losing one's identity to it.

One Flew Over the Cuckoo's Nest is about a group of mental patients. *American Beauty* is about a group of modern suburbanites.

M*A*S*H is about the American military. *The Godfather* is about a Mafia family. Each has a breakout character whose role is to expose the group goal as a fraud. Jack Nicholson, Kevin Spacey, Donald Sutherland, and Al Pacino, respectively, carry this role in these films.

The reason I've dubbed these stories Institutionalized is that the group dynamic these tales tell is often crazy and even self-destructive. "Suicide Is Painless," the theme song of *M*A*S*H*, isn't so much about the insanity of war as the insanity of the herd mentality. When we put on a uniform, be it the uniform of the Army or a comfortable cotton shirt with a little polo player over the pocket, we give up who we are to a certain extent. And these movies are all about the pros and cons of putting the group ahead of ourselves. Again, this is a very "caveman" kind of story. Loyalty to the group sometimes flies in the face of common sense, even survival, but we do it. And we have done it forever. To watch others fight that battle, just like we do every day, is why this genre is so popular... and so *primal*.

Often movies of the Institutionalized category will be told from the point of view of a newcomer. He is us — a virgin who is new to this group and who is being brought into it by someone who is more experienced. Jane Fonda in *9 to 5* and Tom Hulce in *Animal House* are examples. For any world in which the technology, lingo, or rules are not familiar to the average viewer, these characters can be invaluable relayers of exposition. They can literally ask "How does that work?" and allow you to explain the importance to everybody. It's a way to show what is often a "crazy" world to us civilians.

Ultimately, all the stories in this category come down to a question: Who's crazier, me or them? All one need do to understand how sacrificing oneself for the group can be an insane proposition is to check out Al Pacino's face at the end of *Godfather 2*. Here is a guy who has committed suicide for the good of the family and "tradition." And look where it got him. It is just as shocking as Kevin Spacey's last-minute discovery in *American Beauty* and mirrors, almost exactly, Jack Nicholson's blank post-operative expression in *Cuckoo's Nest*. Why? Because it's the same movie, with the same message, told in extremely different and moving ways.

But they all work for a reason.

Because each movie followed the rules.

And they gave us the same thing... only different.

SUPERHERO

The "Superhero" genre is the exact opposite of Dude with a Problem and can best be defined by its opposite definition: An extraordinary person finds himself in an ordinary world. Like Gulliver tied to the beach by the Lilliputians, a Superhero tale asks us to lend human qualities, and our sympathy, to a super being, and identify with what it must be like to have to deal with the likes of us little people. No wonder so many brainy geeks and teens read comic books! They don't have far to go to get in sync and identify with what it's like to be so misunderstood.

This genre goes beyond stories about guys in capes and tights, however. It is more than the Marvel universe or the DC Comics characters. *Gladiator* and *A Beautiful Mind* (both Russell Crowe vehicles — another *hmmm, interesting*) are good examples of human superheroes that are challenged by the mediocre world around them. In both those films, it is the tiny minds that surround the hero that are the real problem. Don't they get it? Well, no they don't. That's why being "special" is so difficult. *Frankenstein*, *Dracula*, and *X-Men* are the same in this regard. Ultimately, all superhero tales are about being "different," a feeling with which even we Lilliputians can identify. Born into a world he did not create, the Superhero must deal with those who are jealous of his unique point of view and superior mind. And from time to time we all feel this way. Anybody who's ever been shot down at the PTA or sneered at for bold thinking in a meeting at work can identify with Frankenstein's monster being chased by an angry mob of mouth-breathers with pitchforks and torches.

The problem of how to have sympathy for the likes of millionaire Bruce Wayne or genius Russell Crowe, is solved by stressing the pain that goes hand-in-hand with having these advantages. It's not easy being Bruce Wayne. The poor guy is tortured! And while it might be cheaper to get therapy (if he can afford a Bat-utility belt, he can certainly pay 150 bucks an hour for a shrink), Bruce Wayne is admirable because he eschews his personal comfort in the effort to give back to the community. This is so often why the first movie in a Superhero series succeeds and ones that follow don't (such as *Robocop 2*). The creation myth that begins each Superhero franchise stresses sympathy for the Superhero's plight. Once established, filmmakers forget to re-create that sympathy and draw us into the human side of the Superhero again. (*Spider-Man 2* avoids this mistake and, not surprisingly, was a smash hit.)

In truth, we will never truly understand the Superhero. Indeed our identification with him must come from sympathy for the plight of being *mis*understood. If you are writing a Superhero movie, a wide range of tales are available for dissection. It's a long-standing story type for a reason: It gives flight to our greatest fantasies about our potential, while tempering those fantasies with a dose of reality.

HOLLYWOOD'S DIRTY LITTLE SECRET

I'm sure having reviewed this list of genres you're not only seeing why so many movies are structurally identical to others, but have had many "Eureka!" moments when you're convinced that outright "stealing" has been perpetrated.

And guess what? You're not so wrong to think that.

Look at *Point Break* starring Patrick Swayze, then look at *Fast and Furious*. Yes, it's the same movie almost beat for beat. But one is about surfing, the other is about hot cars. Is that stealing? Is that cheating? Now look at *The Matrix* and compare and contrast it with the Disney/Pixar hit *Monsters, Inc*. Yup. Same movie. And there's a million more examples: *Who Saved Roger Rabbit?* is *Chinatown*. *Blank Check* is very similar to *Home Alone*. In some instances, the stealing is conscious. In others, it's just coincidence. But very often the reason it happens is that story templates work and they work for a reason that *must* be repeated. Each of these movies is an example of successful storytelling. Several are huge hits. Do you think anyone is complaining that *Fast and Furious* ripped off the story beats of *Point Break*? Did anyone notice but you and me? Doubtful.

The point I'm trying to get across here is — it works. And it works for a reason. Because the laws of physics that govern storytelling work every time, in every situation. Your job is to learn *why* it works and how these story cogs fit together. When it seems like you're stealing — don't. When it feels like a cliché — give it a twist. When you think it's familiar — it probably is, so you've got to find a new way. But at least understand why you're tempted to use the cliché and the familiar story. The rules are there for a reason. Once you get over feeling confined by these rules, you'll be amazed at how freeing they are. True originality can't begin until you know what you're breaking away from.

SUMMARY

The topic of genre dictates the categorizing of movies. But instead of typical categories such as Romantic Comedy or Heist Movie, we've created 10 new ones that define story types. These categories are all you need for now to help you identify the story mechanics of the movie idea you're working on. You will not need to find exclusions to them.

Or have I written those words prematurely?

You are a screenwriter. And as I said in Chapter One, all good screenwriters are bullheads. So I know what your response to the hard work and years of experience that went into what I've just related to you is: *What about the exceptions?* What about *Breakfast Club?* Huh? Is that Rites of Passage or Institutionalized? (Answer: Institutionalized). Oh, yeah, well what about *Rain Man?* Is that a Golden Fleece or a Buddy Love movie? (Answer: Buddy Love). Okay smart guy, what about Ben Stiller's *Zoolander*???? (Answer: It's just a bad movie!! Actually, it's one of my favorite bad movies. But it's also a great example of... the Superhero genre.)

If you're looking for the exceptions to the rules, you're missing the point of this chapter, which is to use categorizing as a storytelling tool. You *must* know movies. But you can't know them all. So this is a way to start. Take the script you're working on and try to find what category it's most like. Maybe you have moments in your script that borrow from all the categories? Maybe you start off your screenplay telling one type of story and end up telling another. That's fine, too. (I mean, **at the end of the day**, I doubt you'll sell that script, but we all have to learn the hard way. We're screenwriters! Pain is the game!)

The point is to be well-versed in the language, rhythm, and goals of the genre you're trying to move forward. If you know what genre you're in, learn its rules and find what's essential; you'll write a better and more satisfying movie.

And have a better chance to sell it.

What's so great about these genres is how inspiring they are — at least to me. Seeing these genres laid out, and seeing their heritage — often going back to very ancient and familiar tales — tells me that the job of "Give me the same thing... only different" is not new. *Jaws* is just a retelling of the ancient Greek myth of the Minatour or even the dragon-slayer tales of the Middle Ages. *Superman* is just a modern *Hercules*. *Road Trip* is just an update of Chaucer's *Canterbury Tales* — isn't it? To not know the roots of the story you're trying to create, either from the last 100 years of movie storytelling or the last thousand, is to not honor the traditions and fundamental goals of your job.

"Give me the same thing... only different" then is what storytelling has *always* been about. But it's the way we put new twists on old tales, bring them up to date, and give them a spin that's meaningful for our contemporaries. It's a skill we must master and apply to all aspects of the craft. And in the next chapter, we'll discuss how to take all this wonderful background and draw out the most important part: the hero.

EXERCISES

1. Pick up the movie section of your newspaper. Review each of the movies available and decide what genre they fall into. If you go see that movie, compare and contrast it with the other movies in that genre. Were you drawn to it because of the type of movie it is?

2. Grab your handy *TV Guide* and go to the movie loglines. Going down the list to check films you've seen, write what genre each falls into. (Using the categories above, simply assign a number to each movie you've seen.) Does it work? Does every movie listed fall into a genre?

3. For the movie idea or script you're working on now, decide what category it falls into. Then make a list of other movies in that genre. As homework, go to your local Blockbuster and see how many of these are available. Make notes about how they compare and contrast to each other. Can you better explain what type of movie your idea or finished script is part of?

4. Finally, for those of you who love to find exceptions to the rules, make up your own genre and give it a name. Find three other movies in that genre. Can you find five? Maybe you've discovered a *new* genre!

If you come up with a brand new genre category, use my e-mail address found in the exercise section of Chapter One and send it to me. If it's really a good one, I may even include it in subsequent editions of this book.

3 IT'S ABOUT A GUY WHO...

The next step in figuring out what your movie is about is to figure out *whom* it's about.

As my wise old father used to say, "Tell me a story about a guy who..."

And after the concept, whenever I hear a screenwriter wind up to pitch his movie idea, somewhere in there I better hear some version of: "*It's about a guy who...*"

Why is this?

Well, it's like anything connected with trying to communicate an idea. The "who" is our way in. We, the audience, zero in on and project onto the "who" whether it's an epic motion picture or a commercial for Tide detergent. The "who" gives us someone to identify with — and that someone doesn't even have to be human. Why do mascots and spokespeople like the Jack character in all those Jack-in-the-Box commercials — or any talking corporate icon for that matter — draw us into the "story" of the product being sold? It's because it's easier to communicate an idea when someone is standing there experiencing it for us. And whether we're watching *Lawrence of Arabia* as Lawrence tries to figure out how to attack Acaba "...*from the land!*" or a Tylenol commercial in which a busy Soccer Mom wonders when her headache will go away, the principle of involving us in the story is the same.

As screenwriters with a great idea for a movie, the job of creating heroes that will lure an audience into our world is unique. We have to create audience stand-ins that resonate for our target market AND serve the needs and goals of our story. And it starts from the very beginning with that great logline that hooks us with some*one* to identify with as much as some*thing*. This is why in any logline, any good logline, there will always be a couple of adjectives involved: A risk-averse teacher who... an agoraphobic stenographer who... a milquetoast banker who.... This also goes for the antagonist who now must be described as an overprotective cop, a megalo-maniac terrorist, or a homicidal baker. So let's add a few things to our list of what the "perfect" logline must include to be truly compelling:

> An adjective to describe the hero
> An adjective to describe the bad guy, and...
> A compelling goal we identify with as human beings

By giving us even these thumbnail sketches of whom we are going to be following — as well as the bad guy who is trying to block our hero from achieving his goal — we get a better snapshot of what is involved so we can latch onto, get interested in, and follow the story. But how are we going to do all that? How are we going to sat-isfy our great story AND create the "right" characters to sell it?

WHO IS THIS ABOUT?

Every movie, even ensemble pieces like *Pulp Fiction* "starring" John Travolta or *Crimes and Misdemeanors* "starring" Woody Allen, has to have a lead character. It has to be *about* someone. It has to have one or two main people we can focus our attention on, identify with, and want to root for — and someone who can carry the movie's theme.

As important as creating this type of hero is, and singling him out even if we're writing an ensemble piece, the hero isn't always the first thing we think of, or the way we come at creating a "can't lose" movie idea. I hate to admit it, but I rarely begin writing any movie with the "who" in mind. More often it's the idea first. And if the hero is a part of the idea — well, that's just gravy. Many will tell you differently, and this is only my approach, but I think the "who" has to serve the "what is it?" — not the other way around. And once you have that golden idea, that winning pitch, that perfect hook, and don't quite yet have the "who," it's time to go to work to enhance the idea with the right characters, especially the hero of the story.

It's all about making the "What is it?" work better.

In many cases, the key to figuring out whom this story is about and what type of person is leading the action is right there in your log-line. In the scripts I've sold, many times the initial concept gave me the roadmap and all I had to do was clarify. In *Poker Night*, a comedy Colby Carr and I sold to Disney, the pitch *is* the characters: "A hen-pecked husband finally gets the house to himself one weekend and loses it in a poker game to an unscrupulous gambler." It's "*Risky Business* with a Dad." Need I say more? To service that concept all we had to do was play with the balance of the hero and the villain — and make it about Dad's journey from henpecked to empowered.

Another comedy we came up with and sold to Universal, called *Third Grade*, has an equally simple premise. This is a story about an adult man who has to go back to third grade. After being caught in a speed trap in front of his old school, the hero is ordered by the judge to be sent back to third grade to learn some manners. Easy concept, right? But who is the best person to put in this situation? What person would offer the most comic conflict given that punishment? What hero would offer "the longest journey" and need to learn the biggest lesson? *Any takers?* Well, in the development process it became clear. The guy who needs that lesson most is someone who has yet to grow up. On the outside he is a successful businessman, a guy up for a promotion at his work — designing violent video games for kids (ironic, no?) — but who has yet to learn the basics of Human Being School.

This is a guy who *needs* to go back to third grade, but doesn't know it yet. And only this adventure will give him the comic lessons he so richly deserves. It's a sweet little movie idea, the poster is inherent in the premise; it's a guy in an Armani suit and a cell phone squeezed into a tiny desk surrounded by out-of-control eight-year olds and maybe a "Kick Me" sign taped to his back. Get it? Well, of course you do. But the gimmick of sending someone back to third grade wouldn't mean anything unless we figured out the perfect hero to take that journey.

AMPING UP THE LOGLINE

Many times, your great initial idea will only give you a hint of what has to be done to create the hero that sells your idea best. To make the idea work, very often you have to play with the characters in order to give your hero the most conflict, the longest journey, and the most primal goal to "amp up" the idea for maximum impact. To make this clear, let's look at our loglines cited in Chapter One and tinker around with other possible "whos" for these ideas.

In *4 Christmases*, all I know is that the two leads are a young couple. They both come from families of divorce and re-marriage — thus the problem of having to see all four of their families on

Christmas Day. My guess is that this is a couple that wants to be together forever, but is having problems at the get-go. They eschew their families and the problems they grew up with; they don't want to get divorced. But maybe it's not all peaches and cream: They're newlyweds! So this day will be a test for them. Do they want to go the way of their parents? Or do they want to go their own way, form a permanent bond, and never get divorced? Granted, I have not read the script. I have no idea what the writers chose to do, but that's the way *I'd* go.

And suddenly, given this very deep and primal urge, the urge to stay committed and be in love forever despite their families, this couple is worth rooting for. That's a movie I'd like to see because those are characters I want to see win. So swiftly, this "easy" premise has real meaning. We have not only identified the "right" characters for this story, but given them a built-in, Alpha-Omega journey to take in the course of this movie. Now the story IS the characters. *And you thought it was just a funny poster!*

In *Ride Along*, part of the pitch, part of the mental picture that makes the idea crackle for me, is the adjectives. A "risk-averse" teacher goes on a ride along with his brother-in-law, an "over-protective" cop, and the goal is primal: the love of the woman they both care about. Those adjectives tell me exactly where this story is going. It's a trial by fire for the teacher: Is he brave enough to overcome his fear and win the hand of his fiancée in the "real" world of manly cops? If he loves her, he will.

But now let's take that same ride-along idea and try some different characters in their places. What if we could do anything with this basic premise? What if the young man who is wooing the sister is not a teacher but an ex-Green Beret? Well, now it's a different movie. It warps the way it plays out in my mind. Now to make the comic conflict come to life, you make the cop the scaredy-cat. He's

Barney Fife and his future brother-in-law will be teaching *him* a thing or two between reminiscences of the Gulf War and a few demonstrations of his "thousand-yard stare." And odds are the ride along would be the ex-Green Beret's idea. Suddenly it's a *very* different movie, isn't it? But it's another way to go. It just shows how you can have a good idea — and absolutely wreck it with the wrong characters. To me, the original idea works best.

In the example of *The Retreat*, again the adjectives come into play to tell us the writers most likely did it right. The way they have it "cast" now, it's about a wet-behind-the-ears (read: young) company employee's first taste of corporate life at a weekend retreat — and someone's trying to kill him. Funny! But let's play around with the character to see other ways they could have gone with this same premise. What if the person going on the retreat is 65, has been at the company for 20 years, and is about to retire? Okay. So now it's about a company "downsizing" its employees for real before they can collect their retirement benefits. Same idea basically: a corporate retreat; a series of murder attempts; a paranoid who doesn't know why he's being targeted. But the journey's a lot different... and so is the moral. And so is the audience: *no one* will show up for that movie. At best it's an Indie starring Jack Lemmon, and Jack is, well, dead.

The point is that amping up a great logline with the hero who makes the idea work best is how the idea comes to life. And let's be clear, the trick is to create heroes who:

> Offer the *most conflict* in that situation
> Have the *longest way to go* emotionally and...
> Are the most *demographically pleasing*!

On this last point, I have particular experience now that I am over 40. Nowadays, I must always catch myself when thinking of my movie heroes. In my mind *everyone* is 40. And the heroes (in my mind), the ones that I am personally drawn to anyway, are now all "existential heroes" — a little world-weary and yet bravely wise. *Yeah! Right!* And the audience that's going to show up for that movie is... well, A.W.O.L. to be honest. (But, if it gets made, the French will hail me as a genius.)

Whenever I find myself drifting into thinking about writing starring roles for Tim Allen, Steve Martin, or Chevy Chase, I catch myself and realize where I am: youth-obsessed Hollywood. Those guys are fine in ensemble, as part of a four-quadrant family pic, great, but as the lead? Never. Okay, rarely. My solution, once I do catch myself and give up on trying to change things, is to make that great character with the existential dilemma a teenager, and make that married couple who's having a crisis a *twenty-something* married couple. This is the crowd that shows up for movies. These are the heroes the audience likes to see onscreen at their local Cineplex.

Why fight City Hall?

The age of characters I think up is my particular blind spot; you have yours. But keep in mind what our job is here: mass market, high concept poster movies for everybody, all over the world. Do not think that just because you and all your friends prefer something, or are in on a certain trend or fad, or like a type of person, that everyone else will, too. I have actually been pitched a movie that the writer said was a great "Julio Iglesias vehicle" — I swear! — won't *everybody* show up for that premiere? (Mucho doubto.) This is why I stress getting out and pitching your movie ideas to real people in the real world to get their reaction.

This discussion of blind spots reminds me of a favorite story my father used to tell. He worked in Advertising early on and one time was trying to sell a client on buying TV time on Sundays. The client, a wealthy man, balked at this idea and had a very studied reason: "No one stays home and watches TV on Sunday," he explained. "Everyone's out playing polo!"

A lesson in perspective for us all.

THE PRIMAL URGE

As stressed throughout this book, let me just say again:

Primal, primal, primal!

Once you've got the hero, the motivation for the hero to succeed must be a basic one. What does X want? Well, if it's a promotion at work, it better damn well be related to winning the hand of X's beloved or saving up enough money to get X's daughter an operation. And if it's a match-up with an enemy, it better well lead to a life-or-death showdown, not just a friendly spitball fight.

Why?

It's because primal urges get our attention. Survival, hunger, sex, protection of loved ones, fear of death grab us.

The best ideas and the best characters in the lead roles must have basic needs, wants, and desires. *Basic, basic!*

Don't believe me?

Then let's look at our three loglines and take out the primal-ness in each to see how our desire to see each wanes:

What if in *4 Christmases*, the lead couple isn't married? What if they're just friends who grew up together and share Christmas with each other's family every year? Same premise. But take out the sex and what have you got? No stakes. Nothing is on the line. It's still funny. It's still the same idea. But I have no primal rooting interest. *Pass!*

In *Ride Along*, try taking out the sister/fiancée. What if the doofus teacher just signs up for a ride along with a cop — any cop. Well, in this gin-rummy hand of primal-ness I've still got: survival. This teacher still has to make it through the night and there will still be risks to his life. But having the cop's sister/teacher's fiancée as the goal makes the stakes resonate with primal-ness. Again, as in the examples in Chapter Two, it's almost a knight-errant tale, isn't it? But having the princess as the prize makes it work whether it's set in the modern day 'hood or the Middle Ages.

One more. Just to grind it in.

The Retreat. Let's take out the danger. What if there aren't any murders? What if it's all pranks played on the newbie executive. Well, where are the stakes? To make this idea work you must have the threat of death; otherwise it's a corporate training film, or worse, an existential metaphor.

And yes, this is all about your hero. Give him stakes. Real stakes. *Primal* stakes. Stakes that are basic, that we understand. Make the hero want something real and simple: survival, hunger, sex, protection of loved ones, fear of death.

And when it comes to who to cast in your screenplay, we respond best to stories of husbands and wives, fathers and daughters, mothers and sons, ex-boyfriends and girlfriends. Why? Because we all have these people in our lives! You say "father" and I see *my* father. You say "girlfriend" and I see *my* girlfriend. We all have 'em — and it gets our attention because of that. It's an immediate attention-getter because we have a primal reaction to those people, to those words even! So when in doubt, ground your characters in the most deep-seated imagery you can. Make it relevant to us. Make it something that every caveman (and his brother) will get.

Make it, say it with me now... *primal!*

CASTING FOR THE ROLE OF YOUR HERO

One of the pitfalls of being a savvy movie writer is knowing who among the acting set is looking to do what part next. Adam wants to do a drama next — to get *his* Oscar nod. Ditto Jim. Ditto Steve. (After *Lost in Translation,* ditto everybody!) We have also seen everyone's most recent movie, may or may not know what's in production next, and *think* we know who'd be perfect for the movie we are writing.

Let me state here and now: We do *not* know!

This is all a long way of saying:
> *Don't* cast the movie before you've sold the script!
> *Don't* write parts for certain actors!
> *Don't* get married to the idea of one particular actor doing the part — you'll *always* be disappointed.

Rare is the occasion when dream script meets dream cast. And let me give you an example of learning the hard way:

The amazing Sheldon Bull and I wrote a hilarious comedy in 2004. What if the President's helicopter goes down behind enemy lines? And what if he is forced to capture Osama bin Laden — all by himself? That was our premise. It's about a President who finds his "inner leader." It's "*Galaxy Quest* with George W. Bush." Great, huh? We even had a great title: *Chickenhawk Down.* And here's why we did not sell that script: Because there are about two people who can play the part of the President. It's the lead. And there really isn't anyone out there who can "open" that movie. Tim Allen was our first choice. And... *who else?* What we had done was paint ourselves into a corner on casting. Yes, it's funny. Yes, it's a great story. Yes, someday it will get made (by God!) but right now it just sits there. *Hear the crickets?*

We are professional screenwriters and we should have known better. But we got so caught up in our idea (*see!?*) that we didn't think it all the way through. The point is to leave yourself plenty of room for casting. Your leads should be able to be played by many actors and actresses. And they should all be able to "open" the movie. This is yet another reason why young actors are in such demand: They're so damn many of them! And no, you do not know what parts actors are looking for. Even if you hear it from their manager. Even if the actor looks you in the eye and tells you that their next movie, the role he *really* wants, is a comedy where he plays a teacher. He is lying. He is an actor. Lovely, charming people to be sure, but skittish as thoroughbreds.

They do not know what they want to do next.

And neither do you.

ACTOR ARCHETYPES

That said, why is it that certain actors always play certain parts over and over again? As hinted at in Chapter Two, you find throughout cinema history that many of the big stars play one part really well. Think about Marilyn Monroe, Clark Gable, Cary Grant. Now think about Jim Carrey, Russell Crowe, Julia Roberts, and Sandra Bullock. It's not because these are not good actors who can't do more than one type of role, only that what makes movies work to a large degree is our need to be shown certain archetypes onscreen.

And the actors who play these archetypes now are just taking the place of the actors who played the same archetypes years ago.

Isn't Russell Crowe Errol Flynn? (Even geographically?)

Isn't Jim Carrey Jerry Lewis?

Isn't Tom Hanks Jimmy Stewart?

Isn't Sandra Bullock Rosalind Russell?

The reason is that these archetypes exist to satisfy our inner need to see these shadow creations in our brains played out onscreen. It's the Jungian archetypes these actors represent that we're interested in seeing. And if you always remember to write for the archetype, and not the star, the casting will take care of itself. So while this may not be strictly Jungian (even though I got an "A" in Jung) let me instead give you some Snyderian archetypes for your perusal:

> There's the "young man on the rise" archetype — a very American character that includes Harold Lloyd, Steve Martin (in his day), Adam Sandler, and the omni-versal Ashton Kutcher. Horatio Alger-esque, a little dumb, but plucky, this is the type we all want to see win.
> There's the "good girl tempted" archetype — pure of heart, cute as a bug: Betty Grable, Doris Day, Meg Ryan (in her day), Reese Witherspoon. This is the female counterpart of the young man on the rise.
> There's the "imp," the "clever and resourceful child" — Jackie Coogan, MacCauly Culkin, and even their evil opposite, the "Bad Seed," i.e., Patty McCormick.
> There's the "sex goddess" archetype — Mae West to Marilyn Monroe to Bridget Bardot to Halle Berry.

> And the male version, "the hunk" — From Rudolph Valentino to Clark Gable, from Robert Redford to Tom Cruise to Viggo Mortenson to Mr. and Mrs. Diesel's pride and joy, Vin.

And the list goes on. There's the "wounded soldier going back for a last redemptive mission" archetype: Paul Newman, and now Clint Eastwood. There's the "troubled sexpot" archetype: Veronica Lake, Angelina Jolie. And the lovable fop: Cary Grant, Hugh Grant. There's the court jester: Danny Kaye, Woody Allen, Rob Schneider. There's the wise grandfather: Alec Guinness and now — same beard, same robe — Ian McKellen.

There are magic dwarves and tricksters, sidekicks and talking animals, spinsters and wizards, Falstaffs and misers — and they keep on popping up. Over and over again. Same characters, same function for being in the story. Like knowing the history of certain story types, knowing the long line of ancestors your characters descend from is a must.

You don't have to be Joseph Campbell to see that no matter who's hot in *Casting Call*, the archetypes never change. Each one of these archetypes has a story arc we want to see played out again and again. And it's all about matching what we carry in the back of our minds to what we see onscreen. Who deserves to win and why? Who deserves comeuppance and why? And despite the dictates of political correctness, fashion and fad, we still want to see justice meted out for characters we hate and victory granted to those we admire. The stories of these heroes and the mathematical equations that makes their stories work is already sewn into our DNA. Your job, your simple task, is to forget the stars, concentrate on the archetypes, and strive to make them new.

SPECIAL CIRCUMSTANCES

And now, for my bullheads in the audience, let's get to the exceptions. When it comes to creating the linear, straightforward movie hero, we pretty much understand. But what about the special circumstances? What about ensemble? What about biographical movies? What about animated movies where the characters come from non-relevant fairy tales??

Okay.

Yes, there are always special circumstances. But finding the hero in all of these examples is the same method used to find them in any original one-line or spec.

Take biography. You've been handed someone's life story and now have to make a movie out of it. So what if the hero isn't necessarily very likeable? Or what if he or she did things that weren't all that admirable, what then? Let's take a look at *Kinsey*. Those of you who know the story about the famous sex study pioneer, Alfred Kinsey, know that the screenwriter (also the director, Bill Condon) faced a problem. Kinsey was odd. He conducted sex studies on friends and neighbors, spied on his wife, and dabbled with his subjects in ways many might think of as objectionable. Finding the hero in that story also means finding a "bad guy," too. But if they can make a movie out of the life of porn-meister Larry Flynt, the publisher of *Hustler* Magazine, as they did in *The People vs. Larry Flynt*, and make him out to be a hero, well, why not follow the same formula? And that's exactly what Condon did.

The writers of *A Beautiful Mind* faced this same problem with mathematician John Nash and chose to simply fudge some of the facts of his life story to make him more palatable. They dropped certain un-heroic facets of his love life and merged two real wives into one for the sake of movie continuity. This kind of thing, with the guidance of a good errors and omissions attorney, is done a lot.

I myself grappled with a similar dilemma when I was handed the biographical challenge of John DeLorean, the famous automaker and creator of the DeLorean sports car. Imagine my surprise when my research proved him not to be a "Tucker-esque" maverick brought down by the Big Three automakers for his radical ideas but, by some accounts, a con man. All well and good, but who's the hero in that story? My solution was to make the hero the author of one of the books I'd read, a guy who had been inside the DeLorean empire from the start and grew disillusioned by both the man and his "vision." By tracing the rise and fall of DeLorean from this insider's point of view, and showing how *he* could be fooled, it gave the audience the "way in" to that story. I even gave my script the ironic title, *Dream Car.* Your way in to a biography has to pay attention to the same rules of any story: It has to be, first and foremost, about a guy who... we can root for.

Or at least understand.

Ensemble pieces can offer the same dilemma for the screenwriter. And as the examples of John Travolta in *Pulp Fiction* and Woody Allen in *Crimes and Misdemeanors* prove, the hero doesn't always have to be the one with the most scenes. But ensemble does offer a unique challenge of finding your way in. Who is this about, you keep asking, this piece with 12 characters, all with equal screen time?

One of the masters of the ensemble, director Robert Altman, specializes in this. *Nashville, Welcome to L.A.,* and *Shortcuts* offer crisscrossing character sketches with no central lead. But Altman would argue differently. The city of Nashville became the "star" of *Nashville,* and *Shortcuts* and *Welcome to L.A.* "stars" the city of Los Angeles. Granted these are not classic hero's tales, but Altman found his way in and stuck to it. And by creating a new kind of hero to root for, he was true to the moral he wanted to tell.

In ensemble, like any story, the "hero" is usually the one who carries the theme of the movie. When in doubt, ask yourself who serves this function in your movie — who comes up against the others the hardest, and who grows the most? And pretty soon you're asking the same questions you ask when finding the hero of any movie you're writing: Who offers the most conflict? Who comes the farthest emotionally and who is the most likeable, the one we want to root for and see win? That's the one you have to make it "about."

Animated tales based on existing material are often difficult challenges, especially when translating across cultural differences and time. Later we will see how the hero of Disney's *Aladdin* went from being an unlikable street urchin in the original text (though one who was perfectly acceptable to the culture in which he was created) to an affable, modern Surfer dude. Likewise in Disney's *Mulan*, *Pocahontas*, and *The Hunchback of Notre Dame*, the writers were presented with similar challenges and met with mixed results based on changes to the hero — and how his or her story was told. But whether your cast of characters is a pack of prehistoric *Ice Age*-ers or a bunch of idiosyncratic insects (*Antz*, *A Bug's Life*), the process of giving us a winning logline, and the hero to star in it, is exactly the same.

The rule of thumb in all these cases is to stick to the basics no matter what. Tell me a story about a guy who...

> I can *identify with*.
> I can *learn from*.
> I have *compelling* reason to follow.
> I believe *deserves to win* and...
> Has stakes that are *primal* and ring true for me.

Follow that simple prescription for finding the hero of your movie and you can't go wrong. No matter what assignment, material, or sweeping canvas has been handed to you, you find the hero by finding the heart of the story.

SLAVE TO THE LOGLINE

When you have found the perfect hero for your story and nailed down just what his primal goal is, it's time to go back to your logline and add in what you've learned to make it perfect. And if it sounds like I am insisting that you become a "slave to the logline" — well, you're right.

The logline is your story's code, its DNA, the one constant that has to be true. If it's good, if it has all the earmarks of a winning idea, then it should give you everything you need to guide you in writing the screenplay. It is, in short, the touchstone, both for you the writer and the audience you're selling your movie to. If you are true to your logline, you will deliver the best possible story. And if you find yourself straying from it in the middle of the writing process, you better have a good reason.

And this is particularly true when it comes to your hero.

The logline tells the hero's story: Who he is, who he's up against, and what's at stake. The nice, neat form of a one- or two-sentence pitch tells you everything. Nailing it down and sticking to it is not only a good exercise, it will become vital to your story as you continue to "beat it out" and eventually write it. By examining who your hero is and what his primal goal is, as well as the bad guy who is trying to stop him from achieving that goal, you can better identify and expand on the needs of your story. The logline with the most conflict, the most sharply defined hero and bad guy, and the clearest, most primal goal is the winner. And once you identify those characteristics and it works, stick to it. Use that logline to double-check your results as you begin to execute your screenplay. And if you find a better way in the writing, make sure you go back and re-enunciate it. But from beginning to end, making it "about a guy who..." keeps you on track. And the logline helps you continue to double-check your math from initial concept to FADE OUT.

SUMMARY

Finding the hero of your story is the second most important part of coming up with a winning movie concept — winning meaning "one that will sell." Cast and concept is, in fact, the starting point of getting any movie made. "What's it about?" and "Who's in it?" are the first two questions any moviegoer asks, and that goes for everyone else as well, from agent and producer to studio executive. It's how the "who" and the "what is it?" come together in an intriguing combination that makes us want to see this story unfold.

The perfect hero is the one who offers the most conflict in the situation, has the longest emotional journey, and has a primal goal we can all root for. Survival, hunger, sex, protection of loved ones, and fear of death grab us. It is usually someone we can identify with primally, too, and that's why mothers and daughters, fathers and sons, brothers and sisters, husbands and wives make better characters than mere strangers facing the same situations and storylines.

When committing these discoveries to your logline, you must have an adjective to describe the hero, an adjective to describe the bad guy, and a definite and primal goal or setting.

EXERCISES

1. Review your list of movies in the genre you are trying to execute and write out the logline for each. Give attention — and great adjectives — to the type of hero, the type of bad guy, and the hero's primal goal.

2. What actor archetypes can you identify from the list of movies in your genre? What type of character is the lead portraying and what actors from the past could play those parts as well as the modern-day star?

3. Name an ensemble movie and identify its hero. Does every movie have to have a hero? Name other movies where the story required no main hero.

4. Finally, if you feel really daring, try writing a logline for this idea: A guy gets a talking car. Knowing what you know about how to amp up the hero, the bad guy, and the primal goal, write a logline for that idea. And make sure you use adjectives that grab us.

4 LET'S BEAT IT OUT!

Itching to start writing your screenplay?

Of course you are!

Will I let you start writing your screenplay?

Keep itching!

But you certainly are getting closer. And think about all that you've accomplished so far. You've polished your one-line and pitched enough "civilians" to know you've got a good one. You've screened a dozen movies that are in the category of story you're trying to tell. You've come up with the perfect hero and antagonist, and amped up both the hero's primal goal and the conflict in the way of his achieving it. And now it's time to take all that great info you've gleaned about your script and figure out how to write the sucker.

There is no greater thrill when I am working on a newly born movie idea than the battle cry: *"Let's beat it out!"*

It means it's time to put all those great scenes and ideas and characters "up on The Board" and see what goes where, which character does what, and whether you need every scene you've imagined... or have to invent all new ones.

It's time to do the measure-twice/cut-once calculation that will save you time, allow you to pitch "beat for beat" and build the foundation and ironwork of your screenplay.

It's time to talk about **structure**.

STRUCTURE, STRUCTURE, STRUCTURE...

After coming up with the idea, and identifying the "who" in your movie — and who it's for — the structure is the single most important element in writing and selling a screenplay. Good structure is ironclad. And when you sell your script, having a well-structured screenplay will show that you have really done the work in making a blueprint that is solid and sound. The **credit jumpers** can change the order of your scenes; they can erase your dialogue; they can add new characters and take others away — and they will! — but if you've done the work on structure, and know how and why your story works, no matter how they tinker, your screenplay will remain strong.

It will remain yours.

Not to get too self-protective, but a strong structure guarantees your writing credit. More than any other element, the bones of a screenplay, as constructed in the story beats of your script, will be proof to those who decide who gets credit at the Writers Guild of America (WGA) that the work is primarily yours. Talk to any writer whose credit has been arbitrated and they'll tell you. For a spec screenwriter, your guarantee that you stay in the picture, and that the fabulous cash and prizes called **residuals** — which come in lovely lime green envelopes at the most unexpected (and welcome) times — will be yours.

The craftsmanship it takes, the patient work, the magic of story-telling on film, all come together in how you execute and realize structure. It is a skill you *must* know.

I came to structure slowly and late. And mostly I came to it out of desperation. How many meetings did I go to early on where I pitched my movie idea by giving the exec the concept, a few "cool" scenes, and then simply stopped and smiled... because I had nowhere else to go? Gad! I remember the first time I was hired to write a screenplay and the executive asked me about my "Act Break." I had exactly *zero* idea of what this nice person was talking about. This was before I'd even *heard* about Syd Field (whom I consider to be the father of the modern movie template), and when I finally read and digested Field's opus *Screenplay,* I knew I had found something truly career-saving.

Oh! *Three* acts! Imagine that?

And yet, it was not enough. Like a swimmer in a vast ocean, there was a lot of open water in between those two Act Breaks. And a lot of empty script space in which to get lost, panic, and drown. I needed more islands, shorter swims.

Viki King filled in a lot more of that open water for me in a book with the unlikely "Get Rich Quick" title of *How to Write a Movie in 21 Days.* And yet, even with midpoints and B stories, there was still way too much room to screw up.

So I developed my own.

From what I'd seen in movies, read about in screenplay books, and found myself relying on, I developed the Blake Snyder Beat Sheet. I wrote out 15 beats and managed to squeeze them all in on a one page document on which the fifteen islands would fit — flush left.

It looks like this:

THE BLAKE SNYDER BEAT SHEET

PROJECT TITLE:
GENRE:
DATE:

1. Opening Image (1):

2. Theme Stated (5):

3. Set-up (1-10):

4. Catalyst (12):

5. Debate (12-25):

6. Break into Two (25)

7. B Story (30):

8. Fun and Games (30-55):

9. Midpoint (55):

10. Bad Guys Close In (55-75):

11. All Is Lost (75):

12. Dark Night of the Soul (75-85):

13. Break into Three (85):

14. Finale (85-110):

15. Final Image (110):

Isn't this pure? And easy?

I use this simple one-page blank form whenever I have a pitch meeting. I won't let myself go into that meeting until I've filled in every space — and there aren't that many spaces. You can only write one, maybe two sentences explaining what each beat is, and that's perfect. Like the one-line description of the movie as a whole, I learned that if I can't fill in the blank in one or two sentences — I don't have the beat yet! I am just guessing. I am treading water, about to drown. Yet it isn't until I work on the form, and try to fill in those blank spaces, that I even know I have a problem!

The numbers in parentheses are the page numbers where the beats take place. A script in terms of page count should be about as long as a good jockey weighs: 110. Though some dramas run longer, the *proportions* are the same. I want my act breaks, mid-points, and All Is Lost moments to hit their marks. And I insist they do. Take a look at *Blank Check* where, five minutes into the movie, roughly page 5 of the script, the theme is stated loud and clear. Look at where the midpoint, the All Is Lost, and break into three hit. They're perfect, and stayed that way from script to screen because Colby and I worked our butts off to make it so from the first draft of that script to the last. It worked because our structure was sound and we had tried it from every angle to make sure it was sound; it defied those who wanted to overwrite us, because we had nailed the structure.

Some of these terms may be unfamiliar to you. What, you may ask, is "fun and games"? Well that's my name for it. And not to worry, it's found in both dramas and comedies. What is the "Dark Night of the Soul"? Again, another "Eureka!" But a beat you've seen about a million times.

The codifying of these beats is now available to you anytime. The Blake Snyder Beat Sheet (The BS2) is here to help. But before you go off half-baked, or all-baked for that matter, let me explain and give examples of what I mean by each section of the screenplay as outlined in this form.

Do you have a choice in this matter?

No, you do not!

OPENING IMAGE (1)

The very first impression of what a movie is — its tone, its mood, the type and scope of the film — are all found in the opening image. I can think of many great ones: the reckless motorcycle ride through the English countryside leading to the death of *Lawrence of Arabia*; the gated, looming castle behind which lurks the mysterious *Citizen Kane*; and even silly ones like the opening image of *Animal House* — who could forget the motto of Faber College: "*Knowledge is good*" beneath the statue of the Faber College founder? Don't we know what we're in for with all three of these examples? Don't each of these opening images set the tone, type, style, and stakes of the movie as a whole?

The opening image is also an opportunity to give us the starting point of the hero. It gives us a moment to see a "before" snapshot of the guy or gal or group of people we are about to follow on this adventure we're all going to take. Presumably, if the screenwriter has done his job, there will also be an "after" snapshot to show how things have changed. Like many of the beats on the BS2, the opening image has a matching beat: the final image. These are bookends. And because a good screenplay is about change, these two scenes are a way to make clear how that change takes place in your movie. The opening and final images should be opposites, a plus and a minus, showing change so dramatic it documents the emotional upheaval that the movie represents. Often actors will only read the first and last 10 pages of a script to see if that drastic change is in there, and see if it's intriguing. If you don't show that change, the script is often tossed across the room into the "Reject" pile.

So the opening image does a lot. It sets the tone, mood, and style of the movie, and very often introduces the main character and shows us a "before" snapshot of him or her. But mostly what it does is get us to scrunch down in our seats in the movie theater and say: "This is gonna be good!" And since you've just screened a dozen movies like the one you're about to write, you can think of at least six that have standout opening images. All good movies have them.

THEME STATED (5)

Somewhere in the first five minutes of a well-structured screenplay, someone (usually *not* the main character) will pose a question or make a statement (usually *to* the main character) that is the theme of the movie. "Be careful what you wish for," this person will say or "Pride goeth before a fall" or "Family is more important than money." It won't be this obvious, it will be conversational, an offhand remark that the main character doesn't quite get at the moment — but which will have far-reaching and meaningful impact later.

This statement is the movie's **thematic premise.**

In many ways a good screenplay is an argument posed by the screenwriter, the pros and cons of living a particular kind of life, or pursuing a particular goal. Is a behavior, dream, or goal worth it? Or is it false? What is more important, wealth or happiness?

"He who has the gold makes the rules!" Preston's lunkhead brother tells him, and that's the Theme Stated in the first five minutes of *Blank Check*. Is the statement true? That's what the movie will debate.

Who is greater in the overall scheme of things — the individual or the group? And the rest of the screenplay is the argument laid out, either proving or disproving this statement, and looking at it, pro and con, from every angle. Whether you're writing a comedy, a drama, or a sci-fi monster picture, a good movie has to be "about something." And the place to stick what your movie is about is right up front. Say it! Out loud. Right there.

If you don't have a movie that's about something, you're in trouble. Strive to figure out what it is you're trying to say. Maybe you won't know until your first draft is done. But once you do know, be certain that the subject is raised right up front — page 5 is where I always put it.

But make sure it's there. It's your opening bid.

Declare: I can prove it. Then set out to do so.

SET-UP (1-10)

The first 10 pages of the script, or first dozen pages at most, is called the "set-up." If you're like me, and like most readers in Hollywood, this is the make-or-break section where you have to grab me or risk losing my interest. Think of all the good set-ups you've seen in **the first reel** — the first ten minutes — which "sets up" the hero, the stakes, and goal of the story... and does so with vigor!

The set-up is also the place where, if you're me the writer, I make sure I've introduced or hinted at introducing every character in the A story. Watch any good movie and see. Within the first 10 minutes you meet or reference them all. Make sure by your page 10 you have done the same.

The first 10 pages is also where we start to plant every character tic, exhibit every behavior that needs to be addressed later on, and show how and why the hero will need to change in order to win. She's an isolated writer who lives in a make-believe world (*Romancing the Stone*); he's a hip, slick, and savvy foreign-car importer who's as glib as he is cold (*Rain Man*); she's a ditzy airhead who doesn't appear to have much substance (*Legally Blonde*).

And when there's something that our hero wants or is lacking, this is the place to stick the **Six Things That Need Fixing**. This is my phrase, six is an arbitrary number, that stands for the laundry list you must show — repeat SHOW — the audience of what is missing in the hero's life. Like little time bombs, these Six Things That Need Fixing, these character tics and flaws, will be exploded later in the script, turned on their heads and cured. They will become **running gags** and **call-backs**. We, the audience, must know why they're being called back! Look at *Big* and its primary set-up: "You have to be *this* tall to go on this ride." On the list of Six Things That Need Fixing there are other needs besides a height requirement. The kid in *Big* can't get the girl, have any privacy, etc. But in Act Two he gets all those things when he magically turns *Big*. And those call-backs only work because we have seen them in the set-up.

Jeez, but that's a lot of stuff to do in the first 10 pages! But there it is. If you want to play with the *Big* boys, these are the tasks you must accomplish.

One last word on the set-up as it relates to Act One. I like to think of movies as divided into three separate worlds. Most people call these three acts, I call 'em **thesis**, **antithesis**, and **synthesis**. The first 10 pages and the rest of Act One is the movie's thesis; it's where we see the world as it is before the adventure starts. It is a full-fledged documentation of the hero's world labeled "before." There is a calm before the storm in this world, and especially in the set-up. If events that follow did not occur, it would pretty much stay this way. But there is a sense in the set-up that a storm's about to hit, because for things to stay as they are... is death. Things *must* change.

CATALYST (12)

The package that arrives in *Romancing the Stone* which will send Joan Wilder (Kathleen Turner) to South America; the telephone call that informs Tom Cruise his father has died in *Rain Man*; the dinner at which Reese Witherspoon's fiancé announces he's dumping her in *Legally Blonde* — these are the catalyst moments: telegrams, getting fired, catching the wife in bed with another man, news that you have three days to live, the knock at the door, the messenger. In the set-up you, the screenwriter, have told us what the world is like and now in the catalyst moment you knock it all down. Boom!

I frankly love the catalyst moment, and I really miss it when I don't see it done, or done well. *Have* to have it. Like my pet peeve — the lack of decent Save the Cat scenes in hip, slick movies — this is another one that bugs me when it's not there. I like the catalyst moment because — it's life. Those moments happen to all of us. And life-changing events often come disguised as bad news. Like many of the beats in the BS2, the catalyst is not what it seems. It's the opposite of good news, and yet, by the time the adventure is over, it's what leads the hero to happiness.

When I'm writing a screenplay, my catalyst moment will float around for the first couple of drafts. The set-up will be too long, the story is clogged with details, and that page 12 catalyst beat is somehow, mysteriously, on page 20. Well, cut it down and put it where it belongs: page 12. And when you start trimming all your darlings away, you'll suddenly realize that's why we have these little structure maps — all that boring detail was redundant or you weren't very good about showing it economically. The catalyst point is the first moment when something happens! Thank God! And if it's not there, the reader will get antsy. Your coverage will read: "No Plot" because you'll have lost the reader's attention. Page 12 — Catalyst. Do it.

DEBATE (12-25)

This is a section of the script, between pages 12 and 25, that used to really baffle me. When the telegram comes on page 12 informing me that my sister is being held by pirates, I know what I have to do! So why do I, the writer, have to vamp to the Act Break until my hero does what he's supposed to?

The debate section is just that — a debate. It's the last chance for the hero to say: This is crazy. And we need him or her to realize that. Should I go? Dare I go? Sure, it's dangerous out there, but what's my choice? Stay *here*?

My writing partner Sheldon Bull and I have been working on our Golden Fleece movie. In Act One, a kid is kicked out of military school and sent home to find... his parents have moved. Well, the kid's stuck. He can't go back to military school and he can't stay where he is. He knows where his parents moved to, so now it's a decision: Should he go on the road to find them? This is our chance to show how daunting a feat this is going to be. Can you imagine? But since it's a comedy, we've also made it funny. Our kid hero is taken to the edge of town at the end of Act One by a friendly cabbie. The kid looks ahead to a spooky-looking road down which he knows he must travel if he is to find his folks. *Gulp!* But his fear is quickly made light of when he's heckled by a driver passing by. And so, on a fun note, and making a firm decision, off he goes.

Your moment of truth may not be so clear-cut, but it's important to remember that *the debate section must ask a question of some kind*. In *Legally Blonde* the catalyst of the fiancé dumping Elle Woods quickly segues to her solution: Go to Harvard Law. "But can she get in?" That is the question posed in the debate section of that movie. The debate section thus becomes showing how Elle answers that question. And when she manages to zoom her LSATs, create a lascivious admissions video, and get accepted, the answer to the question is clear: Yes! And like the kid hero in our "*Home Alone* on the road" movie, Elle can happily march into Act Two. She has answered the debate question and can now proceed.

BREAK INTO TWO (25)

It happens on page 25. I have been in many arguments. Why not page 28? What's wrong with 30? Don't. Please.

In a 110 page screenplay, it happens no later than 25.

Page 25 is the place where I always go to first in a screenplay some-one has handed me (we all have our reading quirks) to see "what happens on 25." I want to know 1) if anything happens and 2) if this screenwriter knows that something *should* happen. And I mean something big.

Because that's what is supposed to happen... on 25.

As discussed above, the act break is the moment where we leave the old world, the thesis statement, behind and proceed into a world that is the upside down version of that, its antithesis. But because these two worlds are so distinct, the act of actually stepping into Act Two must be definite.

Very often when I am writing a screenplay, my act break will start off vaguely. I'll find that events will draw the hero into Act Two. This is incorrect. The hero cannot be lured, tricked, or drift into Act Two. The hero must make the decision himself. That's what makes him a hero anyway — being proactive. Take *Star Wars*. The event that prompts Luke Skywalker on his journey is his parents being killed, but the decision to "go on the road" is his. Luke cannot wake up on Han Solo's starship wondering how he got there, he has to choose to go. Make sure your hero does likewise.

B STORY (30)

The B story begins on page 30. And the B story of most screenplays is "the love story." It is also the story that carries the theme of the movie. I also think that the start of the B story, what takes place around page 30, is a little **booster rocket** that helps smooth over the shockingly obvious A story act break. Think about it. You've set up the A story, you've put it into motion, now we've had this abrupt jump into Act Two and you've landed in a whole new world. The B story says: "Enough already, how about talking about something else!" Which is why the cutaway is usually in line with the A story... but new in scope.

The B story gives us a breather.

Let's take *Legally Blonde*, for instance. The B story is Elle's relationship with the manicurist she meets in Boston. And it is a much needed break from the A story. We've met Elle. She's been dumped. She's decided to go to Law School. She gets there. And school is tough. Well, enough already, let's have a little time-out! Let's go slightly off theme here and meet someone new. Thus, the manicurist. And yes, while it is not a traditional boy-girl love story, it is in fact "the love story." It's where Elle will be nurtured. It is also the place where Elle confides what she is learning in the School of Hard Knocks she's experiencing at Harvard Law — and the place from which she'll draw the strength she needs for the final push into Act Three and ultimate victory.

The B story is also very often a brand new bunch of characters. We have not always met the B story players in the first 10 pages of the screenplay. We did not even know they existed. But since Act Two is the antithesis, they are the upside down versions of those characters who inhabit the world of Act One. Again, the B story ally in *Legally Blonde* is a perfect example. Isn't Jennifer Coolidge, the wonderful actress who portrays manicurist Paulette Bonafonté, the funhouse mirror version of the girls from Elle's sorority house back at UCLA? This is why the character is so successful. She is a classic anti-thesis creature.

The B story then does a lot. And you must have one. It provides not only the love story and a place to openly discuss the theme of your movie, but gives the writer the vital "cutaways" from the A story. And it starts on 30.

FUN AND GAMES (30-55)
The fun and games section is that part of the screenplay that, I

like to say, provides: **The promise of the premise**. It is the core and essence of the movie's poster. It is where most of the trailer moments of a movie are found. And it's where we aren't as concerned with the forward progress of the story — the stakes won't be raised until the midpoint — as we are concerned with having "fun." The fun and games section answers the question: Why did I come to see this movie? What about this premise, this poster, this movie idea, is cool? When you, the development exec, ask for "more set pieces," this is where I put them. In the fun and games.

This, to me, is the heart of the movie. When I discovered what this section of the screenplay needs to do, and why it's there, it leapfrogged me ahead 10 places. For me it happened in the summer of 1989. And it was a definite "Hazzah!" moment that is rarely so clear. When I was writing my very first draft of *Stop or My Mom Will Shoot!* I was sort of stuck. I had this great premise, which was: "*Dirty Harry* gets a new partner — his mother." But what was that? What was that movie about? What were the dynamics of the comedy? (Many of you I'm sure are *still* asking.) Then one day I was sitting up in my office in the Fithian Building in Santa Barbara, California, and I had a great idea: the world's slowest chase! What if Joe the cop and his Mom are shot at by bad guys? And what if they give chase. But what if, instead of Joe jumping behind the wheel and driving — his Mom does. And she drives like a Mom, complete with holding her arm across Joe's chest when they stop at all the stop signs. When I sold my script and went to my first meeting at Universal, the executive told me that when he read that scene, that's when he decided to buy my script. Why? Because that's when he knew there was something to this idea. I had delivered on the promise of the premise. And where did I put that great set piece? Right where it belonged — in the fun and games section of the screenplay.

This goes for drama as well. The fun and games in *Die Hard* show Bruce Willis first outwitting the terrorists. The fun and games in *Phone Booth* occur when Colin Farrell realizes the seriousness of his predicament. We take a break from the stakes of the story and see what the idea is about; we see the promise of the premise and need not see anything else. I also call it fun and games because this section is lighter in tone than other sections. So Jim Carrey gets to walk around and act like God in *Bruce Almighty*. And Tobey Maguire gets to try out his oddly onanistic super powers in *Spider-Man*. It's also where the buddies in all buddy movies do their most clashing. Get it?

Fun and games.

Learn it, love it, live it.

MIDPOINT (55)

There are two halves in a movie script and the midpoint on page 55 is the threshold between them. We can talk about the importance of the two act breaks, but to me the midpoint is as important, especially in the early going of laying out a script's beats. I have found, in reviewing hundreds of movies, that a movie's midpoint is either an "up" where the hero seemingly peaks (though it is a false peak) or a "down" when the world collapses all around the hero (though it is a false collapse), and it can only get better from here on out. When you decide which midpoint your script is going to require, it's like nailing a spike into a wall good and hard. The clothesline that is your story can now be strung securely.

I made the discovery of how important this midpoint moment is quite by accident. In the early days of my movie-writing career, I used to audiotape movies so I could listen to them in my car when I drove back and forth to meetings between Santa Barbara and

L.A. The bargain-basement tapes I bought (I was dead flat broke at the time) had 45 minutes on each side. By coincidence, the drive between Santa Barbara and Los Angeles is divided evenly by a mountain overpass at exactly the midpoint of the drive. Forty-five minutes from starting each trip, as I hit the top of that hill, side A of each tape ended and I had to turn it over to the other side. One night I taped the old comedy classic *What's Up, Doc?*, directed by Peter Bogdanovich and starring Ryan O'Neal and Barbra Streisand. And I discovered, the next day as I topped the mountain crest, that the movie was perfectly, evenly divided into two halves and that its midpoint was a "down."

The first half of *What's Up, Doc?* ends as fire envelops O'Neal's hotel room. A slow fade brings us to the next day, as he wakes up a broken man, and finds... Barbra Streisand waiting to help him — the fire was, after all, her fault! Imagine the revelation I

What can we learn from creaky old movies? Lots. For example, the classic midpoint as Ryan O'Neal and Barbra Streisand share the nadir moment in *What's Up, Doc?*

experienced as I topped the mountain pass and the first half of *What's Up, Doc?* that I had taped came to an end. The movie had two even halves! The power and the purpose of a strong midpoint was forever clear to me.

After that I began to see how many movies had midpoints that changed the whole dynamic of the film. But the midpoint does more than present an "up" or "down." You will hear the phrase "**the stakes are raised** at the midpoint" in a lot of script meetings. Because they are. It's the point where the fun and games are over. It's back to the story! It's also the point where if you have a "false victory" where, say, the hero has been given an Out-of-the-Bottle bit of magic, he gets everything he thinks he wants. But it's a false victory because the hero has a ways to go before he learns the lesson he really needs. It just *seems* like everything's great.

The midpoint has a matching beat in the BS2 on Page 75 called "All Is Lost," which is described as "false defeat." These two points are a set. It's because the two beats are the inverse of each other. The rule is: It's never as good as it seems to be at the midpoint and it's never as bad as it seems at the All Is Lost point. Or vice versa! In the *What's Up, Doc?* example, Ryan O'Neal actually wins the coveted prize at the All Is Lost moment on page 75. But it is a false victory, tainted by the rogue's gallery of crooks descending on the awards ceremony, and setting the action of Act Three into motion. The midpoint and All Is Lost moments of *What's Up, Doc?* represent those for a "down" midpoint. The midpoint is either false victory or false defeat, and the All Is Lost is the opposite of it.

Don't believe me?

Check out the movies you rented in your genre and see if this midpoint-All Is Lost axis isn't in every single one.

BAD GUYS CLOSE IN (55-75)

The section of script from page 55 to page 75, the midpoint to the All Is Lost, is the toughest part of the screenplay. (There's a hard bit of truth for you!) It never fails to be the most challenging for me, and there's no method to get through it other than to just to muscle your way.

This is where your skills as a bullhead come in handy!

The term "Bad Guys Close In" applies to the situation the hero finds himself in at midpoint. All seems fine, but even though the bad guys — be they people, a phenomenon, or a thing — are temporarily defeated, and the hero's team seems to be in perfect sync, we're not done yet. This is the point where the bad guys decide to regroup and send in the heavy artillery. It's the point where internal dissent, doubt, and jealousy begin to disintegrate the hero's team.

I've never had an easy time with Bad Guys Close In. It's the weakest part of *Blank Check*, and Colby and I were convinced at the time that it was fatal to our story. While writing a teen comedy called *Really Mean Girls* with Sheldon Bull, we had a similarly hard time with this section. (Not to mention the fact that we didn't know Tina Fey was writing *Mean Girls* already!) In our very similar story, four underdog girls decide to fight back against the evil blonde Alpha females in their high school. By midpoint they have "out-bitched" them, sent the mean girls packing, and become the superior clique in school. Well, now what? Sheldon and I didn't have a clue.

We answered that question, after a lot of painful think time, by going back to the basics. The evil girls naturally re-group. We even wrote a very funny scene where we see them do that. Then internal dissent among our heroes begins. Popularity starts to go to their heads, each begins to take credit for their victory, and the question of who is the most popular divides them. By All Is Lost, it's the reverse of the way it is at midpoint — the evil girls resume their "rightful" place, and our heroes depart the field in shame. All is *really* lost.

That simple dynamic took us weeks to figure out. It only seems obvious now. Until we solved it, we didn't know.

That is a classic example of what should happen in the Bad Guys Close In section of any script. The forces that are aligned against the hero, internal and external, tighten their grip. Evil is not giving up, and there is nowhere for the hero to go for help. He is on his own and must endure. He is headed for a huge fall, and that brings us to...

ALL IS LOST (75)

As addressed above, the All Is Lost point occurs on page 75 of a good, well-structured screenplay. We know it is the opposite of the midpoint in terms of an "up" or a "down." It's also the point of the script most often labeled "false defeat," for even though all looks black, it's just temporary. But it seems like a total defeat. All aspects of the hero's life are in shambles. Wreckage abounds. No hope.

But here's my little trade secret that I put into every All Is Lost moment just for added spice, and it's something that many hit movies have. I call it **the whiff of death.**

I started to notice how many great movies use the All Is Lost point to kill someone. Obi Wan in *Star Wars* is the best example — what will Luke do now?? All Is Lost is the place where mentors go to die, presumably so their students can discover "they had it in them all along." The mentor's death clears the way to prove that.

But what if you don't have an Obi Wan character? What if death isn't anywhere near your story? Doesn't matter. At the All Is Lost moment, stick in something, anything that involves a death. It works every time. Whether it's integral to the story or just something symbolic, hint at something dead here. It could be anything. A flower in a flower pot. A goldfish. News that a beloved aunt has passed away. It's all the same. The reason is that the All Is Lost beat is the "Christ on the cross" moment. It's where the old world, the old character, the old way of thinking dies. And it clears the way for the fusion of thesis — what was — and antithesis — the upside down version of what was — to become synthesis, that being a new world, a new life. And the thing you show dying, even a goldfish, will resonate and make that All Is Lost moment all the more poignant.

You'd be surprised where this truism shows up. In the comedy hit *Elf*, starring Will Ferrell, the filmmakers stick exactly to the BS2 and there is even a moment where the whiff of death is clearly seen.

Will Ferrell senses the "whiff of death" as he contemplates suicide in the All Is Lost moment of *Elf*.

In that story, about a human (Will) raised as an elf in Santa Claus's North Pole, Will comes to New York to find his "real dad," James Caan. The hilarious upside-down world of Act Two includes a classic anti-thesis character, Will's love interest, who is working as a "fake" elf in a department store at Christmas time. But later, when it all goes to hell one night for poor Will, when his real father rejects him and the world gets too complicated, we even have a death moment at page 75. Will pauses on a city bridge and, looking out at the water waaaay below, clearly contemplates suicide. When I saw this film in the theater I practically yelled out "See! Whiff of death!" but managed to restrain myself. And yet, there it was, plain as day.

Take a look at your dozen movies you've screened and find the All Is Lost point. Does it have the whiff of death in some aspect? Most certainly it will. All good, primal stories must have this. It resonates for a reason.

DARK NIGHT OF THE SOUL (75-85)

So now you're in the middle of a death moment at the All Is Lost point, but how does your character experiencing this moment feel about it? This question is answered in a section of the screenplay I call Dark Night of the Soul. It can last five seconds or five minutes. But it's in there. And it's vital. It's the point, as the name suggests, that is the darkness right before the dawn. It is the point just before the hero reaches way, deep down and pulls out that last, best idea that will save himself and everyone around him. But at the moment, that idea is nowhere in sight.

I don't know why we have to see this moment, but we do. It's the "Oh Lord, why hast thou forsaken me?" beat. I think it works because, once again, it's primal. We've all been there — hopeless, clueless, drunk, and stupid — sitting on the side of the road with a flat tire and four cents, late for the big appointment that will save our lives. Then and only then, when we admit our humility and our humanity, and yield our control of events over to Fate, do we find the solution. We must be beaten *and know it* to get the lesson.

The Dark Night of the Soul is that point. It's in comedies and dramas because it's real and we all identify. And in a good, well-structured screenplay, it's in there between pages 75 and 85. And thank God, because by page 85, when the hero finally figures it out, we get to see him realize...

BREAK INTO THREE (85)

... Hazzah! The solution!

Thanks to the characters found in the B story (the love story), thanks to all the conversations discussing theme in the B story, and thanks to the hero's last best effort to discover a solution to beat the bad guys who've been closing in and winning in the A story, lo! the answer is found!!

Both in the external story (the A story) and the internal story (the B story), which now meet and intertwine, the hero has prevailed, passed every test, and dug deep to find the solution. Now all he has to do is apply it.

The classic fusion of A and B is the hero getting the clue from "the girl" that makes him realize how to solve both — beating the bad guys *and* winning the heart of his beloved.

An idea to solve the problem has emerged.

The world of synthesis is at hand.

FINALE (85-110)

The finale is Act Three. This is where we wrap it up. It's where the lessons learned are applied. It's where the character tics are mastered. It's where A story and B story end in triumph for our hero. It's the turning over of the old world and a creation of a new world order — all thanks to the hero, who leads the way based on what he experienced in the upside-down, antithetical world of Act Two.

The finale entails the dispatching of all the bad guys, in ascending order. Lieutenants and henchman die first, then the boss. The chief source of "the problem" — a person or thing — must be dispatched completely for the new world order to exist. And again, think of all the examples in the movies you've screened of how this is true. The finale is where a new society is born. It's not enough for the hero to triumph, he must change the world. The finale is where it happens. And it must be done in an emotionally satisfying way.

FINAL IMAGE (110)

As stated earlier, the final image in a movie is the opposite of the opening image. It is your proof that change has occurred and that it's real. If you don't have that final image, or you can't see how it applies, go back and check your math — there is something not adding up in Act Two.

SUMMARY

So now that I've laid out these 15 beats for you, and used examples like *What's Up, Doc?*, I'm sure all you hip, young screenwriting whipper-snappers are saying, yeah, right old man. Maybe this applied in your day, but we don't need it anymore. We eschew the need to "like" a hero (we dig *Lara Croft*!!!) and those boring old story beats are passé. Who needs 'em? What about *Memento*!!

Have I grasped the basic gestalt of your objection?

Existential dilemmas are what close on Saturday night, as the low-performing art house gem *Memento* proves. Gimmick or really dull movie? You decide.

If so, and though I've tried to pepper my examples with many newer movies, like *Legally Blonde*, you still may not believe me when I say this stuff applies. Still. Always.

So for you nay-sayers, who say nay, let me use an example from my genre, PG Comedy, that shows how these beats apply in the modern world you need to master.

Oh, and btw, screw *Memento*!

Let's use a $100 million Box Office (B.O.) hit. Would that satisfy you? Let's look at a great poster and logline, with a great star that satisfies all the beats in the BS2. Let's take a look at the Sandra Bullock comedy, *Miss Congenialty*.

To start, it's got a great title. And its logline — an ugly duckling FBI agent goes undercover as a contestant to catch a killer at the American Miss pageant — certainly satisfies the four elements from Chapter One: irony, compelling picture, audience and cost, and a killer title. Let's see if it beats out according to the BS2?

MISS CONGENIALITY
(A $100 million hit comedy in 15 beats)

Opening Image: *Miss Congeniality* opens on Sandra Bullock's character in flashback as a playground tough. The image is: Sandra surrounded by boys. Sandra is a tomboy and she's beating them up. Sandra has issues. When we CUT TO: The Present, Sandra is still surrounded by boys, still a tomboy, but she's an FBI agent, at home in the world of Men — kind of.

Theme Stated: When Sandra declares that she doesn't need to worry about being "feminine" because she's an FBI agent, that statement is the movie's theme. But is this statement true? We shall see. The movie will explore the subject of femininity. It is an essay on the pros and cons of being tough *and* a woman. Can you be both? That's what this movie is *about*.

The Set-up: By page 10 we have met everyone who will appear in the A story of the movie and "set up" the world. We've met Benjamin Bratt, whom Sandra kind of likes. But she is off his radar; he likes "classy" girls that Sandra scoffs at. We also meet Sandra's boss (Ernie

Hudson) and the world of the FBI. It's tough, a boy's club, and Sandra fits right in. And though she is a wheezing nerd with bad hair and no social life, she *seems* happy — a classic set-up, with a sense a storm's about to hit. It can't stay like this. Stasis equals death.

Catalyst: A classic call to adventure. News comes that there's been a murder threat at the American Miss Pageant. We also meet those in charge of the pageant, Candice Bergen and her son, and their "Bert Parks," William Shatner and his hairpiece — and a very sporty model it is! To stop the murders, they hatch a plan that calls for a female agent to go undercover as a contestant. After going through a database of every available female FBI agent... they pick Sandra.

Let the act break and let the fun and games begin. Ugly duckling Sandra Bullock looks hot, hot, hot in her miniskirt as she strides into Act Two of *Miss Congeniality*.

Debate: But can she pull it off? That is the debate question of this section. It is answered after several funny moments with Sandra's mentor (Michael Caine), who agrees to take on the challenge of turning Sandra into a sexy girl.

Break into Two: Sandra strides from her makeover looking hot, hot, hot in her mini-skirt. Even Benjamin is impressed. Then she stumbles. This isn't going to be easy, but Sandra is ready to try. So let the act break and Act Two begin!

Fun and Games: Classic promise of the premise, including all those funny trailer moments where a pistol-packing FBI agent is undercover at the American Miss pageant. Sandra's water-glass talent show demonstration ends as she leaps off the stage to nab a suspect, etc. The fish is out of water and the clash leads to jokes. This is why we came to this movie. This is what lured us when we saw the poster. And it's fun!

B Story: The love story here is actually between Sandra and the girl contestants. Why? Because the theme of the movie is about femininity and Sandra does not know this world. It is full of funhouse mirror versions of femininity — each contestant has a talent and a quirk and each, to Sandra's surprise, needs and likes her. It is Sandra's interaction with the girls of Girl World that carries the message of the picture and is its heart. And while Sandra also gets to kiss Benjamin by the movie's end, it will be because of the girls that she learns and grows and discovers her feminine side.

Midpoint: The fun and games are over as a new threat to the pageant is announced and Sandra's stakes are raised. We have seen all the fun stuff (Sandra and her water glasses), met the suspects, had the joy of watching a tomboy interact with the girls she once thought odd. Now the real trouble starts.

Bad Guys Close In: Sandra's doubts about her femininity grow, her conflict with her mentor deepens, and, in this case, actual bad guys move closer, unseen in the shadows of the pageant. Though no one has died, there's a list of suspects.

All Is Lost: Told by her boss to stand down, Sandra refuses. She has a lead on a suspect. But her boss delivers an ultimatum: Either quit the case or be fired. Sandra chooses to stay on at the pageant. Thus, she has reached a classic All Is Lost moment: *She is worse off than when this movie started!* The whiff of death is the death of her identity. Without being "the Girl with the Badge" — who is she? Not even her mentor (Caine) can help, but he does give her a last weapon: a new dress.

Dark Night of the Soul: Sandra arrives for the pageant finale and is a total mess. She's lost in the netherworld of being neither FBI agent nor full-fledged woman. What to do?

Break into Three: With help from friends she's made in Girl World, Sandra is put back together by the other contestants for the pageant finale. Embraced by what was once foreign to her, and confident that the girls really care, Sandra is revived. By helping Sandra, the girls also help themselves.

Finale: The pageant itself. A classic bit of synthesis occurs when Sandra hangs in during the talent portion of her show by using her FBI skills on stage with Benjamin. The two worlds are fused together, answering the question raised in Theme Stated: Yes! She can be both tough *and* sexy. Sandra now catches the bad guys, Candice and her son. (Candice's warped view of her own femininity is what caused her to sabotage the pageant.) Sandra has proven herself to be a woman among women. And she's brought the bad guys to justice.

Final Image: *Miss Congeniality* closes with the opposite of the opening image: Sandra is surrounded by women. Sandra is awarded the coveted Miss Congeniality Award by her fellows — quite a change!

The <u>Real</u> Happy Ending: $100 million in domestic B.O.

Now that you know that it works, you'll start to see how these beats can apply to your script.

EXERCISES

1. Type up the BS2 and carry it with you everywhere. Whenever you have an idle moment, think about a favorite movie. Can the beats of that movie fit into neat, one-sentence descriptions of each of the 15 blanks?

2. Go back to Blockbuster (boy, are they tired of you by now) and check out the 6-12 movies in the genre of the movie you're writing. Sit and watch as the beats of these films are magically filled into the blanks of the BS2.

3. For extra credit, look at *Memento*. Yes, it's an entertaining movie; yes, it even falls into the category of genre "Dude with a Problem." Does it also match the beats of the BS2? Or is it just a gimmick that cannot be applied to any other movie? HINT: For all the hullabaloo surrounding *Memento*, guess how much it made?

And if you want to seriously debate the value of *Memento* in modern society, please go ahead and contact me at the e-mail address provided in Chapter One. But be ready for one hell of an argument from me!! I *know* how much *Memento* made.

5 BUILDING THE PERFECT BEAST

If we are very lucky we find a guru. These are people we meet along the way that have more wisdom than we do and, to our surprise, offer to share what they know. Mike Cheda is the first guru I met in the screenwriting business and for 20 years he has continued to amaze me with his ability to spot, understand, and fix the problems of any screen story.

I first met Mike when he was head of development for Barry & Enright. Mike also worked in that capacity for Disney and was VP of Development at HBO and Once Upon A Time Productions. Over the years, Mike has developed hundreds of movie and television projects — often from initial concept to final cut. He has not only been an executive for these and other companies, but is himself a writer (something more development execs should try) whose *Chill Factor* starred Cuba Gooding, Jr. and the Dash Riprock-named Skeet Ulrich.

No matter what incarnation Mike Cheda appears under — executive, writer, or producer — wherever he goes, his magic story touch is the stuff of legend. Of the many scalps on his belt, Mike is the guy credited with cracking the story for the Patrick Swayze movie, *Next of Kin*. Though it was a spec script purchase in the million-dollar range, *Next of Kin* had problems that needed tweaking before it could get a green light — and it was Mike who solved them. Mike even showed me the *place* where this event occurred. One day we were taking a time-out from a story we were trying to break, bowed by despair and self-loathing over not knowing how. While walking through Century City, Mike stopped at the hallowed piece of sidewalk.

It was here, he said, Jacob Bronowski-like, during a similarly meditative walk when his brain was filled with all the wrong ways to fix *Next of Kin*, that he'd come up with the right way. "It just hit me. Cowboys and Indians!" And indeed when he presented this simple construct to the producers of *Next of Kin*, that's exactly what guided the rewrite. In the course of his career, Mike has had many such moments. Like some String Theory physicist, he is always working on perfecting his story skills — often in ways that seem otherworldly, but almost always prove to be inspired.

So when I ran into Mike recently and asked what new ideas he'd come up with, he pulled out an artist's sketchbook from his satchel and opened it with gleeful enthusiasm. The two halves of the sketchpad, its spiral binding running down the middle, offered a larger-than-normal field. Across both pages, he had drawn three straight lines, demarcating four horizontal rows. And in the middle of these four equal rows were cut-out squares of paper, each was a beat of the screen story he was working on.

"It's portable," Mike cackled like a mad scientist.

"Ah!" I said. "The Board."

And we both nodded with the respect.

The Board.

CHAIRMAN OF THE BOARD

The Board is perhaps the most vital piece of equipment a screen-writer needs to have at his disposal — next to paper, pen, and lap-top. And over the years, whenever I've walked into someone's office and seen one on the wall, I have to smile because I now know what it is — and the migraine-in-progress it denotes. Boards come in all types and sizes: blackboards smeared with chalk, cork boards with index cards and pushpins to hold the beats in place, and even pages of a yellow legal pad Scotch-taped to hotel walls while on location — in the attempt to re-work a script on the fly. The Board is universal. And yet of the screenwriting courses I know of, I've never really heard this useful tool discussed.

So damn it, let's talk about it!

I saw my first one on Mike Cheda's office wall at Barry & Enright 20 years ago. *Naïf* that I was — though I'd already been paid actual money to write a few screenplays — I'd never seen The Board, nor could I imagine what it would possibly be used for. Didn't you simply sit down and *start* and let the scenes fall where they may? Didn't you just… let 'er rip?

That's what I always did.

But thanks to the Chairman of The Board, Mike Cheda, I learned not only the vital importance of planning a script by using The Board, but how to use it to supercharge my results. Since that time I have employed it often. In my case, I use a big corkboard that I can hang on the wall and stare at. I like to get a pack of index cards and a box of push pins and stick up my beats on The Board, and move 'em around at will. I have many decks of these index cards, rubber banded and filed by project, of scripts written and yet-to-be. And all I need to do to revisit any of these scripts is take out the pack, deal 'em up on The Board, take a look to know where I left off — and figure out if I need to call Mike.

The Board is a way for you to "see" your movie before you start writing. It is a way to easily test different scenes, story arcs, ideas, bits of dialogue and story rhythms, and decide whether they work — or if they just plain suck. And though it is not really writing, and though your perfect plan may be totally abandoned in the white heat of actually executing your screenplay, it is on The Board where you can work out the kinks of the story before you start. It is your way to visualize a well-plotted movie, the one tool I know of that can help you build the perfect beast.

But here are the most beneficial things about The Board:

> a. It's tactile and...
> b. It wastes a *lot* of time!

The exercise of working The Board uses things other than your fingers on a keyboard. Pens, index cards, pushpins. All things you can touch, and see, and play with at will.

And did I mention how much *time* you can waste doing all this?

You can spend a whole afternoon at Staples picking out just the right-sized board. You can spend the next morning figuring out where it goes on your wall. You can even go mobile with the index cards. You can pop that deck in your pocket, head out to Starbucks, take the rubber band off, and sit there and shuffle your cards for hours, laying out scene sequences, set pieces, and whammies. It's great!

And the best part is, while you're doing all this seemingly ridiculous, time-wasting work, your story is seeping into your subconscious in a whole other way. Have a great piece of dialogue? Write it on a card and stick it on The Board where you think it might go. Have an idea for a chase sequence? Deal up them cards and take a looksee.

And talk about creating a pressure-free zone! No more blank pages. It's all just little bitty index card-sized pages. And who can't fill up an index card?

All well and good but how does it apply to *me*? you ask.

Me! Me! Me!

All right, let's talk about you and *your* Board.

FIRST CARDS FIRST

Once you've bought the size and type of board you feel most comfortable with, put it up on the wall and have a look. It's blank, isn't it? Now take three long strips of masking tape and make four equal rows. Or if you're more daring, use a magic marker instead. Either way it looks like this:

ACT ONE (p. 1-25)
ACT TWO (p. 25-55)
ACT TWO (p. 55-85)
ACT THREE (p. 85-110)

Row #1 is Act One (pages 1-25); row #2 represents the first half of Act Two up to the midpoint (25-55); row #3 is the midpoint to the Break into Act Three (55-85); and row #4 is Act Three to the movie's final image (85-110).

It looks so easy, doesn't it? Well, it is. That's the whole idea. And after a couple of go-rounds using this tool, it will start to feel familiar, too. Soon, like a slot car racetrack, the corners and open stretches of this imaginary concourse will become well-worn and pleasing geography.

You will quickly find that the ends of each row are the hinges of your story. The Break into Two, the midpoint, and the Break into Three are where the turns are; each appears at the end of rows 1, 2, and 3. To my mind, this fits my mental map of what a screenplay is perfectly. And if you buy Syd Field's premise that each of the turns spins the story in a new direction, you see exactly where it occurs.

Now in my hot little hand I also have a crisp, clean, brand new pack of index cards. (Oh, it's fun to unwrap the cellophane!) And now with the help of a fistful of Pentels (*not* a Clint Eastwood movie) and my box of multi-colored pushpins, I'm ready to put up my very first card. To waste as much time as possible, I usually neatly write the title of the movie on one such card and stick it up at the very top and take a step back. In a few weeks, or months, the Board is going to be covered with little bits of paper, arrows, color-coding, and cryptic messages. For now, it's clean.

Enjoy it while you can, lads.

Okay. Time to start.

Although you can write anything you want on these index cards, they are primarily used to denote scenes. By the time we're done, you'll have 40 of these — count 'em, 40 — and no more. But for now, in this rough stage, we'll hang loose. Use as many as you want. And if you run out, you get to go back to Staples and waste more time — so go for it!

What goes on your final 40 is very simple. Each card stands for a scene, so where does the scene take place? Is it an INTERIOR or an EXTERIOR? Is it a sequence of scenes like a chase that covers several locations? If you can see it, write it with a magic marker: INT. JOE'S APARTMENT – DAY. Each card should also include the basic action of the scene told in simple declarative sentences. "Mary tells Joe she wants a divorce." More specific information will be noted later. For now, the average beat or scene looks like this:

INT. JOE'S APARTMENT - DAY
Mary tells Joe she wants a divorce.

+/-
> <

In any storytelling venture, the most burning ideas you have for scenes are what must be laid out first. These are scenes you're sure are going to go into your movie. It's what made you want to write this puppy in the first place. For me, most often, these are funny set pieces, followed by that great scene where we introduce the hero, and maybe the finale. Well, write each idea on a card and stick it up on The Board where you think it goes. It may wind up in another place or may be cut out, but damn it feels good to get those scenes off your chest. Yup. They're up there, all right.

And look at what you have.

What you have is a whole lot of blank space. Gee, aren't you glad you didn't start writing? All those really great ideas that were burning to be written don't feel as big as you thought they were. And the story doesn't seem so likely to write itself once the ideas are written down and put up on The Board. The great way the movie starts or the chase at the middle or the dramatic showdown that felt so full, so easy to execute in your head, isn't all that much stuff when you see it there naked. Up on the board, they're just a small part of the whole. But if you want to see these wonderful scenes come to life — and have a *reason* to live — work must be done. Now the hard part begins.

THE MAJOR TURNS

The next cards you really must nail in there are the hinge points of the story: midpoint, Act Two break, Act One break. Since you have the advantage of the BS2 you know how vital these are. And even though you may come at it a whole other way, I always try to figure out the **major turns** first.

I start with the midpoint. As discussed in the previous chapter, it's an "up" or "down." Either your hero (or heroes) reach a dizzyingly false victory at page 55 or an equally false and dizzying defeat. In most cases, nailing the midpoint will help guide you — and it is the one decision you must make before you can go on. Most people can nail the break into Act Two. The set-up you've got, and the adventure, or at least the beginning of it, is the movie in your head. But where does it go from there? The midpoint tells you. And that's why figuring it out is so important.

With the midpoint nailed, the All Is Lost is not too hard to figure out. It's the flip of the midpoint. What about the "up" or "down" of the midpoint can be reversed to create its false opposite? And though it may take you some time to adjust both, give it a try. If you nail these two points, the Break into Three is usually cake. Now your board is starting to flesh itself out. It should look more like this:

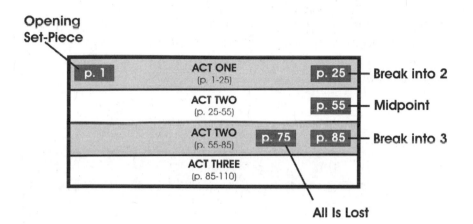

OVERLOADED ACTS AND BLACK HOLES

For me, my biggest problem is mistaking the cards for something other than beats of the story, something other than actual scenes. This is especially true in the early going as I lay out the set-up and the action of the first act. I give myself three or four cards for the first 10 pages, that's three or four scenes to get me to the catalyst. But a lot of times what I'll see spread out there are seven or eight cards with things like "the hero is a wrongly accused felon" next to "the hero is a saxophone player." Well, these are not scenes, this is backstory. And these cards will eventually be folded into one card labeled "Meet the Hero" during an actual scene in which he walks into a room and we see him for the first time.

As stated in the previous chapter, a lot of this backstory, these character tics and set-ups need to be... set up. And all your great ideas will go on cards and just pile up here like BMWs on the 405 at rush hour. Never fear, it will all be pared down eventually. Point is to get it all out. This is the time to try anything, think of *everything,* and stick it all up there to see what it looks like.

More confusion comes when scene sequences are laid out up on The Board. Though things like "a chase" involve many scenes and can range through indoor and outdoor set-ups, it's actually only one beat. So what usually happens is you have five, six, seven cards that are a sequence. Well, these will fold into one eventually but for now will look like this:

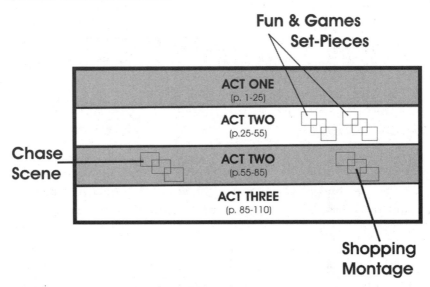

One great part about using The Board is the easy way you can identify problem spots. When you have a **black hole** — a place in your script that you can't figure out how to connect one chunk to another — you know it, 'cause it's staring you right in the face. All you have to do is look at The Board and cry. And believe me, those black holes just sit there and taunt you, hour after hour, day after day. "What's wrong, Blake? Can't figure it out? Got a little... *STORY* problem?" But at least you know where it is and what has to be done to fill in the blank spots. You've got nine to 10 cards per row that you need to fill. And you have to figure it out.

THE ETERNALLY LIGHT ACT THREE

The funny part about laying out these cards is: In the early going, you almost always have a light Act Three.

It's usually two cards. One labeled "the Hero figures out what to do now" and the other labeled "the Showdown."

Ha! Kills me every time I see it.

And you always keep putting off fixing this.

Not to fear.

Eventually this too will give way. Your mind will flood with ideas and Act Three will begin to fill up. If not, then go back to Act One and look at all your set-ups and the Six Things That Need Fixing. Are these paid off in Act Three?

If not, they should be.

What about your B story? Whether it's the true love story or the thematic center of the movie, this must be paid off, too. In fact, the more you think about tying up all the loose ends, the C, D, and E stories, recurring images, themes, etc., the more you realize all the screenplay bookkeeping that has to be accounted for in Act Three. Where else can it be done? (What? You gonna pass out pamphlets at the movie theater?)

And what about the bad guys? Did you off all the lieutenants on your way to killing the über-villain? Did all of the hero's detractors get their comeuppance? Has the world been changed by the hero's actions? Soon you will find your Act Three crowded with cards and ideas to fill up the final scenes. Nine or 10 cards will be required to do this.

Guaranteed.

COLOR-CODING

Now here's a really cool thing. And it wastes a lot of time! But it's also important. How each character's story unfolds and crosses with others needs to be seen to be successfully worked out. This is where your Pentels come in. Color-code each story. See what Meg's story cards look like written in green ink and Tom's story cards are like written in red. And when you put them up on The Board, you can see at a glance how the stories are woven together — or if they need to be re-worked. This is one instance where you will not know how you lived *before* you used The Board. And seeing these beats up there makes you realize what a potential nightmare it would be to try to figure this all out while writing. Screenplays are structure. Precisely made Swiss clocks of emotion. And seeing your different colored stories woven together here makes you realize how vital this planning can be. But color-coding can be used for other things too:

> story points that follow and enhance *theme* and *repeating imagery* can be color-coded.
> *minor character arcs* can be traced with your Pentels.
> *c, d, and e stories* can get the color-code treatment.

And once you have your multi-colored cards in place, you can step back and see the genius (!) of your design.

All this is intended, of course, to ultimately save you time. What could be worse than being in the middle of actually writing your screenplay and dealing with these placement questions? It's a lot easier to see and move cards around on a board than chunks of your own writage that you've fallen in love with. It's a lot harder to kill your darlings by then. By organizing first, the writing is more enjoyable.

STRIPPING IT DOWN

Forty cards. That's all I'm going to give you for your finished board. That's roughly 10 cards per row. So if you've got 50 or if you've got 20, you've got problems.

Most likely you will have more than you need. And this is where the rubber meets the road, when you must examine each beat and see if the action or intent can't be folded into another scene or eliminated altogether. Like I mentioned previously, I usually have problem areas. Set-up is a biggie for me. I have 20 cards sometimes in the first row. I think there is so much to say, so much I'm not getting across that I overcompensate. But then I look at how these beats can be cut out or folded into others. If I'm honest, if I really admit that I can live without some things, it starts to cut down. I get it down to nine cards.

And that's perfect.

I will also have a lot of sequences. Like chases or action set pieces that stray all over the place. This is easy to fix. Simply write CHASE on this section, no matter how many scenes, and consider it one beat. Usually that's all it is as far as advancing the plot is concerned.

In areas where I'm light, like the problem area of Bad Guys Close In, I usually cut myself some slack. And in some spots, where I know I don't have all the answers, I occasionally even leave it blank and hope for a miracle during the writing process. But in the back of my mind, I know these areas will have to be addressed at some point. Laying it out lets me know where the trouble spots are.

+/- AND ><

Now that you have your 40 cards up on The Board and you're pretty sure this is how your story goes, you think you're done, but you're not. Here are two really important things you must put on each card and answer to your satisfaction before you can begin writing your screenplay:

One is the symbol +/-. The other is the symbol ><.

These two symbols should be written in a color pen you have not used and put at the bottom of each card like this:

INT. COFFEE SHOP - DAY
Bob confronts Helen about her secret.

+/-   Bob starts out hopeful, ends up disappointed.

> <   Bob wants to know secret; Helen can't tell him.

The +/- sign represents the emotional change you must execute in each scene. Think of each scene as a mini-movie. It must have a beginning, middle, and an end. And it must also have something happen that causes the emotional tone to change drastically either from + to − or from − to + just like the opening and final images of a movie. I can't tell you how helpful this is in weeding out weak scenes or nailing down the very real need for something definite to *happen* in each one. Example: At the beginning of a scene your hero is feeling cocky. He's a lawyer and he's just won a big case. Then his wife enters with news. Now that the case is over, she wants a divorce. Clearly what started as a + emotionally for your lawyer hero is now a − emotionally.

Believe it or not, an emotional change like this must occur in *every* scene. And if you don't have it, you don't know what the scene is about. Until you figure out the emotional change for each of the 40 cards using this simple +/- code, don't start. And if you can't figure it out, throw the card away. Odds are it's wrong. And while many, like Robert McKee, believe these +'s and −'s must be strung together +-/-+/+-/-+/+- to butt up against each other in an undulating wave of emotional highs and lows, I think that's taking it a little far. It's enough to know something has to change in each scene and to show it.

The other symbol, ><, denotes conflict. To understand what the conflict is, I always like to think of a scene like this: As the lights come up, two people walk into a room from opposite doors, meet in the middle, and begin to struggle past each other to reach the door on the other side. They each enter the scene with a goal and standing in their way is an obstacle. *That's* conflict. And whether it's physical or verbal or simply a guy who really needs to pee and must get to a bathroom soon or else!, that conflict must be foremost on your mind when you conceive each scene. The basic set-ups of Man vs. Man, Man vs. Nature, and Man vs. Society that you learned in high-school English class can all be applied here.

When each scene opens, you must know what the main conflict of that scene is and who is bucking against whom. Each person, or entity, has an agenda. What is it? And how does it collide with the person or entity he or she must get past? The symbol >< on the bottom of each card must be filled in with who each of the players is in each scene of conflict, what the issue is, and who wins by the end. If it's more than one person or issue, you've got a muddy conflict. And your scene is probably muddy, too. Only one conflict per scene, please. One is plenty. And whether it's a large issue or a small one, something physical or something psychological, it must be there. Every scene. Every time. If you can't find a conflict, figure out a way to create one.

The reason having conflict is so important and must be in every scene is, once again, very primal. (There's that word again.) And thinking primally, by having conflict in every scene, guarantees that you will keep the audience's attention. Why? Well, we like to see people in conflict. Conflict gets our attention. Why is wrestling the longest running drama on TV? It's about as basic an entertainment as you can get: DEATH! Two people trying to *kill* each other. Why do most movies have a romance? Again, the conflict is eternally primal and fascinating: SEX! Two people trying to *bed* each other. At its core, every scene in your movie must be as basic as this in order to get and keep the viewer's attention. If you don't have the players in the > vs. < match-up your scene represents, you don't have the scene yet. So...

Find the conflict... or reassess... or dump it.

And if you do, don't cry, it's only a card.

READY TO LET IT FLY...

By the time you're done, you should have nine cards in row #1, nine in row #2, nine in row #3 and nine in row #4 — wait! That's only 36 cards. Well, I'm giving you four extra for those scenes I know you can't live without. Stick these wherever you like — we don't have to be *that* precise. But 40 is all that you get... or need.

You do not get points for having the most perfectly laid out Board. And as much fun as it is to play with these cards, and fantasize about the ebb and flow of your story, there is a point where you must ask yourself, "Am I in the Board-building business or am I a screenwriter?" If your Board is too perfect, or if you spend too much time trying to make it so, then you have left the world of preparation and entered the Procrastination Zone. Well, don't. In fact, I always like to start writing when I'm coming up on the end of finishing The Board, just before it gets too perfect. Like a Jell-O® mold that's not quite set, you wanna start *before* it hardens. By then I'm obsessed with pushpins and index cards and I know it's time — to stop.

To me, always, speed is the key. I want to figure this all out so I can get to the writing. And once I have my 40 beats laid out and my +/- and >< done on each card, I know I've done as much as humanly possible to prepare. And now I'm ready to put away my pushpins and cards and pens... and start typing. (Suddenly typing will feel GREAT!)

The work on The Board is important. But it's a trick I play on myself, an exercise in storing moments, rhythms, scenes, and scene sequences in my brain. It allows me to play with these elements without commitment to any of them. I must always be willing to throw it all away as I begin the writing process. How many times have I gotten in there and started writing and dumped every preconceived notion of what I had? How many times have I fallen in love with a minor character that has risen to become one of the leads who wasn't even mentioned in the outline of my Board? Well, *lots* is the answer. That's what happens. What The Board will do for you is prepare the battlefield, allow you to test your theories, grind in certain notions, and minimize others.

FINAL WORDS ON THE SUBJECT

Truth is when you write FADE IN: The Board means nothing. But I hope the things I've tried to get across to you will still be burning in your brain and will stick with you. These are: the necessity of hitting your act break on page 25, hitting the midpoint and All Is Lost *hard*, and the need to have conflict in *every* scene. Even if these things are all that you remember as you get lost in your story, you'll be in great shape. These islands in a sea of uncertainty are important to keep in sight as you begin to write.

And it's all designed to get you to THE END.

The blessing of having this handy guide up on the wall of your work room is: If you do get lost, if you can't figure out what happens next, you can always go back to The Board and get back on track. *The worst thing that can happen in screenwriting is to not finish.* Half-written screenplays *never* sell, that's for sure. And working out The Board in advance is your best guarantee that this won't happen.

CHECKING IN WITH MY SECRET WEAPON

Of course when *I'm* really stuck, I call Mike Cheda.

"Miiiike," I whine. "I don't know what happens in Bad Guys Close In, can you take a look?" I then e-mail my notes to Mike and go have an expensive lunch up at The Eurotrash Café on Sunset Plaza, confident that SOMEONE is working on my project — even if it's not me. Mike is the one person I know in Hollywood who actually reads the material you send him and knows how to fix it! He will even give you detailed notes. And he's a real smart aleck too — which I like (it keeps me on my toes). But you know you're in trouble when you come back from your expensive lunch, having flirted with the Euro-Hostess and feeling *very* good, and you call Mike and the first thing out of his mouth is: "You're kidding, right?"

If you too want to reach Mike Cheda for screenwriting advice, you can do so on the Internet at *www.mikecheda.com*, where for a fee of $500 Mike will read and analyze your screenplay. I think this is the bargain of the century and I am always telling him to up his price. He should be charging $5,000 per script if you ask me. A story about Mike in *Creative Screenwriting* Magazine referred to him as "The Dr. Phil of screenwriting." Another understatement. To me, he'll always be the guy who taught me everything I know.

For free.

SUMMARY

So now you know everything about your movie that you need to start writing your screenplay. If you have held off long enough on your movie idea to do the steps I have suggested, you're ready to write FADE IN: and begin.

Are you excited?

You should be. But let's just make sure you're set by going over the "Get Ready for Your Deep-Sea Dive" Checklist:

1. You have come up with a great idea. And I mean it's killer! You have a killer title, a KILLER logline, and you've tested it on friends and strangers, and every one of them can't wait to see your movie!

2. You have done your homework on genre. You've figured out what your movie is most like and screened every relevant Hollywood film in the past 20 years. You know what the filmmakers did right, what they did wrong, and more importantly how your movie will be a step forward and be the same thing... only different. And you are convinced you've got something new!!

3. You have figured out the perfect hero to take this journey. This is the character that offers the most conflict in that situation, has the longest way to go emotionally, and is the most demographically pleasing! And you've given your hero a primal goal and a real bad guy who wants to stop him from achieving it!!!

4. Finally you have beat out your movie using the BS2 and have put up all those great scenes on The Board, tried many ideas, themes, and storylines, and have whittled it all down to 40 actual scenes with each scene indicating its emotional change from beginning to end (+/–) and what the conflict is in each (><)!!!!

Man, are you ready!! What's stopping you?

While you go off and start writing your screenplay, we'll be waiting for you and rooting you on. We'll be the guy up on the dock that feeds the oxygen tube down to you, the deep-sea diver, as you descend into the depths of your subconscious mind. Make sure that in your life you too have similar support from friends and loved ones. Because as you drop into the depths of your story, trying to capture the thoughts and the feelings you need to accomplish your mission, you have to trust that those up in the real world are supporting you and are watching your back. It's weird down there! You'll see all manner of wondrous and strange things, be amazed by what you're capable of handling, and surprised by how great an experience it can be. But it's also dangerous; doubt and anxiety will plague you, and, like the bends, it will cause you to see fearful things that aren't even there. In order to get through to THE END you've got to have someone back on land that you trust, that's supporting and nurturing your effort.

Whether you have that situation in your life or not, *we'll* be up on the dock waiting for you. And wishing you well. We who write screenplays want to see you win, and win *big* time, and we know exactly what you're going through down there and want you not to worry. So as you descend into the murk, as ready as you'll ever be, we wish you good hunting. And while we wait for you to come up, we'll kill a little time and talk about some fun things in screenwriting.

Good luck, and Godspeed, Screenwriter.

EXERCISES

1. Take the beat sheet from one of the movies you have screened from your genre and write the beats on index cards. Put the cards up on The Board, or if you have not gone to Staples yet, try the portable version.

2. Find several scenes from your favorite movies and break them down according to their +/– values. How does the scene start emotionally? How does it end emotionally? Are these opposite emotional beats?

3. Now take the same scenes and test them for >< conflict. Who or what are the opposing forces on each side of the conflict? Who wins? Do your favorite scenes in these movies have the most conflict? Is bigger conflict better?

6 THE IMMUTABLE LAWS OF SCREENPLAY PHYSICS

The real inspiration for this book started with one simple desire: I had a whole bunch of snappy rules for screenwriting and I wanted to get credit for coining them.

There! I said it.

These are little ironclad laws that my screenwriting buddies and I have collected over the years. And I love 'em! It's because, to me, screenwriting is a science as much as an art. It's quantifiable. The rules that govern it are constants, and in some cases eternal (see Joseph Campbell).

Like any study of the craft of storytelling, these truths become apparent as you watch movie after movie. And when one of these immutable laws is suddenly clear to you, the urge to yell "Eureka!" is overwhelming. You want to plant your flag on it and claim it as your own.

Of course it's not. These laws can't be "discovered." They're truths that existed way before you or I came along. Yet every time another one pops into my lexicon, I am *thrilled*.

I love these Immutable Laws of Screenplay Physics so much I wanted to make this whole book about nothing else — but common sense intervened. To get to the good part, I had to explain the screenwriting process, from idea to execution, in order for anyone to understand what I was talking about.

And aren't you glad I did?

But even though this is the dessert part for me, the fun, the *raison d'etre* of the whole operation, there are some of you out there who will still want to pee on my Pop Tarts. Yes, there will be a few among you who will doubt my rules!

You are the type of person who bucks the system, who wants to make your own rules, thank you very much. When told that you *can't* do something, you want to do it all the more.

You know... a *screenwriter!*

To those of you who doubt me, bravo! But at least let me show off a little bit here, let me run amok — ego-wise — and tell you how smart I am to have uncovered these things before you go and stomp them dead. And try to remember the value of knowing these is so that you *can* override them. Before Picasso could dabble in Cubism, he had to become a master of basic drawing. It gave him credibility and authority. So for you budding Picassos, a few of my screenwriting basics:

SAVE THE CAT

I've found that Save the Cat, the title of this book and the screenwriting law it denotes, is amazingly controversial! Though many screenwriters I've shown this manuscript to are impressed with its premise, a few are horrified with this one idea and find it my least best thought. Many think my example of Save the Cat found in *Sea of Love* (as detailed in the Introduction of this

book) is old-fashioned and the worst piece of advice in an otherwise helpful primer. Not only that, they find the idea of making
the hero "likeable" to be cloying and dull, an exercise in kissing up
to the audience.

To review, Save the Cat is the screenwriting rule that says: "The
hero has to *do* something when we meet him so that we like him
and want him to win." Does this mean that every movie we see has
to have some scene in it where the hero gives a buck to a blind man
in order to get us onboard? Well no, because that's only part of the
definition. So on behalf of my hypercritical critics, allow me a
mid-course addition:

The adjunct to Save the Cat says: "A screenwriter must be mindful
of getting the audience 'in sync' with the plight of the hero from
the very start." To explain what I mean, let's take a look at a movie
that definitely does *not* try to kiss up to the audience: *Pulp Fiction*.
Scene One of *Pulp Fiction*, basically, is where we meet John
Travolta and Samuel L. Jackson. These are the "heroes." They are
also drug-addicted hitmen (with really bad haircuts). Quentin
Tarantino does a very smart thing when we meet these two
potentially unlikable guys — he makes them funny. And naive.
Their discussion about the names of McDonald's hamburgers in
France is hilarious. And sort of childlike. We like these guys from
the jump — even though they're about to go kill someone — we are
"with" them. In a sense, Tarantino absolutely follows the STC
rule. He knows he has a problem: These two guys are about to do
something despicable. And in the case of Travolta, he will become
one of the main characters of the film, a guy the audience *must* like
in order to root for him. Well, after meeting these two crazy
knuckleheads, we *do* like them. They're funny. Instead of risking the
audience's good will by making them existential hard asses without a
soul, screenwriter Tarantino, in his own way, makes them sorta
huggable.

Save the Cat!

The problem of making anti-heroes likeable, or heroes of a come-uppance tale likeable enough to root for, can also be finessed with STC. The Immutable Laws of Screenplay Physics tell us that when you have a semi-bad guy as your hero — just make his antagonist *worse*!! A little further on in the introductory scene of *Pulp Fiction*, Tarantino does just that. Before he and Samuel Jackson reach the door of their victims, Travolta raises the specter of their Boss, and tells a story of how an underling, like himself, was thrown out of a window for giving the Boss's wife a foot massage. This is just another example of a great STC trick: When your hero is slightly damaged goods, or even potentially unlikable, make his enemy even more horrible. If you think Travolta is bad, well, look at the Boss. Travolta is a doll compared to *that* guy. And BINGO! The scales of whom we like versus whom we hate are adjusted to perfect balance. Let the rooting begin!

The problem of unlikable heroes even occurs in nice family films. My favorite Save the Cat example, and one that I repeat way too often, comes from the Disney movie, *Aladdin*. When developing this hit film, Disney found they had a real problem with the likeability of the main character. Go back and read the source material. Aladdin, as described in the original stories, is kind of a jerk. Spoiled. Lazy. And, to make matters worse, a thief! Thank God, Disney had Terry Rossio and Ted Elliott on their team. Rossio and Elliott are to me the two best screenwriters working in Hollywood today. (And so unsung! Where is their publicist?!?!)

What these two crafty writers did was give Aladdin an introduction that solved the problem and was a classic example of Save the Cat. In that $100+ million hit, the first thing we see Aladdin *do* is impishly steal food because, well, he's hungry. Chased by Palace

Guards with scimitars all over the market square (a great way to introduce *where* we are too, btw), Aladdin finally eludes them. Safe in an alley, he is about to chow down on his stolen pita, when he spots two starving kids. And, what a guy! Aladdin gives his falafel snack to *them*. Well now we're "with" Aladdin. And even though he's not quite the original thieving, layabout character, we're rooting for him. Because Rossio and Elliott took time to get us in sync with the plight of this unlikely hero, we want to see him win.

The point of all this is: Care! Though you don't have to have a scene in every movie where the hero literally saves a cat, helps an old lady across the street, or gets splashed by water at the street corner to make us love him, you must take the audience by the hand every time out and get them in sync with your main charac-ter and your story. You must take time to frame the hero's situa-tion in a way that makes us root for him, no matter who he is or what he does. If you don't, if you go the *Lara Croft* route and *assume* we'll like your main character — just cuz — you're not doing your job. And even though some movies do this and get away with it, it doesn't make it okay. Or good and careful storytelling.

Am I off the hook on this now, fellow screenwriters?

THE POPE IN THE POOL

The Pope in the Pool is more of a trick than a rule, but it's a fun one that I love to talk about and one that I see done onscreen all the time. It is also one of the first insights passed on to me by Mike Cheda, script master.

Your problem is: How to bury the exposition? **Exposition** is backstory or details of the plot that *must* be told to the audience in order for them to understand what happens next. But who wants to waste time on this? It's boring. It's a scene killer. It's the worst part of any complicated plot.

So what's a good and caring screenwriter to do?

Mike Cheda told me about a script he once read called *The Plot to Kill the Pope,* by George Englund, which did a very smart thing. It's basically a thriller. And the scene where we learn the details of the vital backstory goes like this: Representatives visit the Pope at the Vatican. And guess where the meeting takes place? The Vatican pool. There, the Pope, in his bathing suit, swims laps back and forth while the exposition unfolds. We, the audience, aren't even listening, I'm guessing. We're thinking: "I didn't know the Vatican had a *pool?*! And look, the Pope's not wearing his Pope clothes, he's... he's... in his bathing suit!" And before you can say "Where's my miter?" the scene's over.

The Pope in the Pool.

The Pope in the Pool comes up all the time, but I've written one scene using this trick that I'm really proud of. It was in a script called *Drips* that Colby Carr and I wrote and sold to Disney. A comedy (duh!), *Drips* is about two dumb plumbers who are tricked into an oil-stealing plot that is to unfold beneath the streets of Beverly Hills. Suckered into the heist by a Beautiful Girl, Plumb and Plumber are invited to the Girl's Boss's house where the Bad Guy will explain the heist and essentially lay out the plot of the movie. He will describe how our two plumbers will be required to tap into an old oil well beneath the house, and connect the runoff to the sewers beneath the city which inevitably lead to the sea and the Bad Guy's waiting oil tanker. (Trust me, it's possible.) And yet we risked the audience's attention as we forced them to sit through this potentially joy-killing exposition.

Our solution? The Pope in the Pool.

In the scene, before the meeting starts, we show our two doofus heroes having an iced-tea drinking contest to show off for the Beautiful Girl — whom they both like. By the time the meeting begins, they both need to pee. Really badly. The humor of the scene comes from them sitting there, legs crossed, trying to concentrate on the Bad Guy's powerpoint demonstration while all manner of pee-inducing images are seen around them. Out the window, lawn sprinklers go on and the neighbor's dog takes a big, relieving wiz on a bush. And in the room, the Girl pours a nice, tall glass of iced tea for herself from a crystal pitcher. Seeing these things, our two heroes are going slowly cross-eyed with discomfort, all while the Bad Guy drones on with the vital heist information.

We got the information across... and it's hilarious.

In the *Austin Powers* films, Mike Meyers has done us one better by naming a character Basil Exposition (Michael York), whose sole purpose is to tell the boring backstory to the British super spy... and us. Every time Basil appears we know we're going to get a dose of elucidation, but revel in the fact that *they* know *we* know it's boring and have made light of that fact.

There are dozens of examples of the Pope in the Pool and now that you are aware of it (if you weren't already), you can come up with new ways to bury the backstory. Whether it's the two funny guards scene in *Pirates of the Caribbean*, where we get the lowdown on Jack Sparrow, or the batting cage scene in a thriller like *A Clear and Present Danger*, the Pope in the Pool gives us something to look at that takes the sting out of telling us what we need to know.

And does so in a lively and entertaining way.

Good trick. Thanks, Mike Cheda.

DOUBLE MUMBO JUMBO

Double Mumbo Jumbo is a favorite. It is also a rule you and I can't break, even though we see it broken all the time!

I propose to you that, for some reason, audiences will only accept *one piece of magic per movie*. It's The Law. You cannot see aliens from outer space land in a UFO and then be bitten by a Vampire and now be both aliens *and* undead.

That, my friends, is Double Mumbo Jumbo.

Yet despite the fact that it throws a big ol' *sabot* into the machinery of the audience's brain, even though Double Mumbo Jumbo is logically wrong, it's done all the time.

My favorite example is *Spider-Man*. Why is it that you went willingly to see this movie, it became a big hit, and yet when it comes on cable you don't want to see it again?

Can't be the actors; we love Tobey and Kirsten and Willem. Can't be the special effects; swinging through the city on a spider web is cool! I propose that our interest vanishes around the middle of the movie when the Green Goblin first appears. That's where I always lose interest anyway.

Why? Double Mumbo Jumbo.

The makers of *Spider-Man* ask us to believe two pieces of magic in one movie. Over here on this side of town, a kid is bitten by a radioactive spider and endowed with superhero powers that combine nuclear fusion and arachnia. Okay. I'll buy that. But then over on the other side of town, Willem DaFoe is getting a whole other set of magic powers from an entirely different source when a lab accident transmutes him into The Green Goblin. So... you're saying that we have a radioactive spider bite AND a chemical accident?! And both give one super powers? I'm confused! They're straining my suspension of disbelief. They're breaking the reality of the world they asked me to believe in once already. How dare they! Like Save the Cat, when I see the DMJ rule violated I get mad. It's sloppy. It's a product of moronic creativity. Yet in the world of comic books, you're sort of excused.

Double Mumbo Jumbo is also in another big hit, one that doesn't get let off the hook because it's from a comic book. In M. Night Shyamalan's *Signs*, we are asked to believe that aliens from outer space have invaded Earth. Apart from the really embarrassing finale in which a super intelligent alien is dispatched with a base-ball bat ("Swing away, Merrill!" is now my favorite bad line), the movie is *about* Mel Gibson's crisis of faith in God.

"Swing away, Merrill!" A super-intelligent alien who has traveled light years in a highly advanced spacecraft is dispatched with a Louisville Slugger in M. Night Shymaylan's *Signs*.

Huh?!

I'd say proof of an alien intelligence outside our solar system sorta trumps all discussion about faith in God, don't you think? But M. asks us to juggle both. And it's a mess.

My guess is M. started his script with his one piece of magic — aliens, crop circles — and realized we'd seen that. In an effort to make his alien movie different, he tried to make it meaningful. Okay. But in doing so, he also made it muddy. The minute aliens arrive, the problem of Mel Gibson's crisis of faith is, well, ridiculous. You want to see a miracle? Look out the window — ALIENS HAVE LANDED, MEL!!!! Because what M. is asking us to balance in our minds is a debate about whether or not God AND Little Green Men exist.

Well, God and aliens don't mix. Why? Because it's two sets of different kinds of magic. It's Double Mumbo Jumbo. And if you don't believe me, try substituting the word "Allah" for the word "God" and see if your brain doesn't melt.

So unless you too have a hit movie in your back pocket, or a comic book you must translate to screen, don't try it.

Only one piece of magic per movie, please.

It's The Law.

LAYING PIPE

Minority Report starring Tom Cruise did it. So did *Along Came Polly* featuring Ben Stiller and Jennifer Anniston. Each of these movies did something that risked failure. And once I point out their flaw, you will see that perhaps they did more than risk it. In my opinion, both these movies came up short because the filmmakers went long. They forgot one of the immutable laws of movie physics we screenwriters live by:

Audiences can only stand so much "pipe."

What is pipe? And what is the risk of laying too much of it?

Well, let's take a look at *Minority Report*, the big-budget movie based on yet another work by sci-fi writer Philip K. Dick. In death, Dick has become the "go-to guy" for source material that has resulted in such hits as *Blade Runner* and *Total Recall*. In *Minority Report* the hook is typically Dickian, but in this case, setting up the premise almost kills the story. *Minority Report* is about future crime. And we see exactly how this works in the opening scene of the film. A homicide is about to take place, and since Tom Cruise is in charge of the task force that monitors these future crimes, we see him spring into action and stop the murder. In the next scene, we jump to the politics involved in how this operation works. Tom, we learn, is under investigation by Colin Farrell. We even meet the three "pre-cognitives" who lie in a tub of water and predict the future. We also see that in his personal life, Tom lost his child and has some kind of drug problem. We also meet Tom's mentor (Max Von Sydow) whom we don't totally trust. Okay. All well and good. But by the time the writers lay out the pipe required to set up this story, I am personally exhausted! It's interesting, but what's the point? Where is this going?

The story finally gets under way when Tom receives the latest future news and lo! the criminal pegged is himself. Knowing that the pre-cogs are never wrong, Tom must find out how and why this mistake has been made — and stop the murder that he supposedly will commit. The clock is running; and so are we. There's only one small problem: By the time this plot point happens, we are 40 MIN-UTES INTO THE MOVIE! It took *40 minutes* to set up this story and explain to the audience what it's about. It took *40 minutes* to get to the hook, which is: A detective discovers he is the criminal.

Say it with me now, fellow students: *That's a lot of pipe!!*

In *Along Came Polly*, we find the same problem. In order to get to risk-averse divorcee Ben Stiller falling in love with crazy girl Jennifer Anniston, the writer also has a lot of pipe to lay. We have to see Ben marry his first wife, follow them on their honeymoon, and watch as Ben catches her in the arms of their scuba instructor. Sure it's funny. And we'll put up with a lot when it comes to any movie that Ben is in. We love Mr. S! But the screenwriter and director (same guy — the funny and talented John Hamburg) risks our attention by laying a ton of story points to get to the reason we came to see this movie: Ben Stiller dating Jennifer Anniston.

In both *Along Came Polly* and *Minority Report*, the laying of all that pipe — a necessary thing to set up the story — risks our attention and, I believe, contributes to a lesser movie-going experience. By needing so much backstory to set up the movie, the whole story has been torqued out of shape.

To be honest, laying pipe is something about which I am hyper-aware, and in many cases I have stopped writing stories due to the pipe required to set them up. *Blank Check* has a little bit more pipe up front that I am comfortable with. There is way too much 'splainin' to do to get us to the point where our hero, Preston, walks into the bank with his blank check for a million bucks. A lot of back and forth. A lot of pipe. It's not quite fatal, but almost. There's about a half a beat more movie in Act One than I like. And it risks the audience's patience. *Get to it!!* I hear them screaming. And as screenwriters, we need to be aware of risking the attention spans of our audience. The point is if you find yourself with a set-up that takes more than 25 pages to introduce, you've got problems. We call it "laying pipe"; the audience calls it "I want my money back!"

BLACK VET A.K.A. TOO MUCH MARZIPAN
When dealing with conceptual creativity, an offshoot of the Double Mumbo Jumbo rule is a rule I call Black Vet.

You often fall in love with certain elements of a movie idea and cling to them. You can't let go. You're Lenny in *Of Mice and Men* and you're going to squeeze that little rodent to death. And usually when you find yourself in this situation, you must stop. This is when the Black Vet rule allows you to step back from the concept.

What is Black Vet?

Better to tell you where it came from. In the 1970s, comedian and now actor/writer/director, Albert Brooks, made several film parodies for *Saturday Night Live*. In one of his best, a piece that tweaked the nose of NBC and the silliness of network programming, Brooks did a hilarious fake promo for several upcoming shows that would be seen that fall on NBC.

One of these was called *Black Vet*. In unctuous "NBC — Be There!" style, it showed a black actor who played a veterinarian cavorting with animals at his clinic. But this guy *also* has a past in the military. The punchline came when the narrator announced the name of the show and its fake promo line: "*Black Vet: He's a veteran and a veterinarian!*" Hilarious! But it is also so close to a real show on real TV, so much about the desperation of Hollywood types trying to squeeze 10 pounds of shit into a five-pound bag, that I found it to be brilliant. And I personally never forgot it."Black Vet" is a joke, and yet you'd be surprised how often we creative folks get caught piling on our great concepts. Like eating too much marzipan, a little goes a long way where ideas are concerned. And more does not always mean better.

In my career, my favorite example of this came when I was working with my first writing partner, the quick-witted and entrepreneurial Howard Burkons. We were young and energetic writers with a lot of great ideas — and a lot of bad ones. But Howard and I achieved early success and even earned our WGA cards while working together, a huge step forward for us both. Because we were working in TV, we had a TV series idea, and a good one I thought. Set in the 1950s, it followed the adventures of a blacklisted private eye. We called the show *Lefty*. Get it? Lefty referred to his political affiliation, but sounded tough and very '50s. Okay. But Howard and I killed the idea when Howard insisted we also make our hero left-handed. And maybe, Howard suggested, he could also be an ex-boxer, a left-handed ex-boxer! So he's a Communist *and* an ex-boxer *and* he's left-handed? I kept asking. And Howard thought that was great. Well... to my mind it was "pick one." To Howard it was a matter of milking the idea for all it was worth. And while I usually trusted Howard's instinct on this stuff — Howard is brilliant when it comes to conceptualizing and a much smarter marketer than I — I just didn't get it.

It was Too Much Marzipan.

It was Black Vet.

What we had succumbed to was getting stuck on a good idea. And it's easy to do. You like that? Well, hell you'll like it even more if I just add a couple of more scoops of the same thing on top, right? Well, no. To this day, whenever I talk with my pal Howard, he insists he was right about *Lefty*. Me? It's a whistle I don't hear. Still! But it makes a great rule of screenwriting and creativity: Simple is better. One concept at a time, please. You cannot digest too much information or pile on more to make it better. If you do, you get confused. If you do... stop.

WATCH OUT FOR THAT GLACIER!

Very often when bad guys are involved, they will be way off screen somewhere, far away from our hero, and "closing in." Sometimes they close in so slowly, the noose tightens so lackadaisically, you want to yell at the screen:

Watch Out for That Glacier!

Well, I do anyway.

That's how the "danger" is coming toward your hero: s-l-o-w-l-y! One inch per year. That's how unthreatening your supposedly threatening horror is. And if you think this doesn't happen to the big boys as well as you and me, you're wrong. Slow danger happens to good movies all the time.

Just check out Pierce Brosnan in *Dante's Peak*, one of two volcano movies that came out in 1997, presumably to cash in on all that Mt. St. Helen's buzz. And here's what *Dante's Peak* is about: See that volcano? It's gonna blow any minute!! That's it! And that's all it is. A volcano is about to erupt and no one believes the handsome scientist (Pierce Brosnan), so we sit there and wait for him to be right (we saw the trailer). Well, while we're waiting at least we can look at Brosnan and think: Yeah, Sean Connery *was* better.

And check out Dustin Hoffman in *Outbreak*. Now there's a dull movie! Basically, it's about a super Ebola virus that comes to the U.S. and Hoffman's attempt to find the cure. But while we're waiting, that virus is slowly, slowly, *really* slowly headed our way. It's a Monster in the House movie basically, but in *Outbreak*, they have to create the "house" by quarantining a small town and introducing us, in thumbnail sketches, to the people who live there so we'll care if they die. Of course, we don't meet them until like page 75!! But so what?! We gotta do *something* while we're waiting for this Butterball to baste and for Dustin to catch an infected monkey, which, if I remember correctly, is the D or E plot of *Outbreak* and... Man! How did these guys get talked into this?

It even happens in Westerns. In *Open Range*, Kevin Costner's and Robert Duvall's cowboy buddy gets killed by the bad guys on about page

20, at which point Kevin and Robert sit there on their horses and talk about the bad guys and how they're gonna go get 'em, yup they sure should go get 'em... *for about an hour and a half!* If you ever wondered how the West was won, apparently it happened very slowly.

See, even bright people think the slow encroaching danger of hot lava headed your way, oh about by Thursday or so, will get our emotions stirring. But lo! it does not.

Danger must be *present* danger. Stakes must be stakes for people we care about. And what might happen to them must be shown from the get-go so we know the consequences of the imminent threat. If not, you are violating the Watch Out for That Glacier rule. Here is a list of other "glaciers" that approach slowly or are too remote, unthreatening, or dull:

> An evil Slinky
> Snails armed with AK-47s
> A foreclosure letter sent from Siberia
> A homicidal one-legged Grandmother
> A herd of angry turtles
> Locusts

Even if you have a catchy title, do not write movies with these "bad guys." Okay, well, unless the locusts are biologically-altered locusts that like to eat human flesh!!

Then we'll talk.

THE COVENANT OF THE ARC

The Covenant of the Arc is the screenwriting law that says: Every single character in your movie must change in the course of your story. The only characters who don't change are the bad guys. But the hero and his friends change a lot.

And it's true.

Although I hate the term "arc" because it's gotten so overused by development executives and How to Write a Screenplay authors, I do like what it stands for. **Arc** is a term that means "the change that occurs to any character from the beginning, through the middle, and to the end of each character's 'journey'" (another est-y kind of term). But when it's done well, when we can chart the growth and change each character undergoes in the course of a movie, it's a poem. What you are saying in essence is: This story, this experience, is so important, so life-changing for all involved — even you, the audience — it affects every single person that is in its orbit. From time immemorial, all good stories show growth and track change in all its characters.

Why is this?

I think the reason that characters must change in the course of a movie is because if your story is worth telling, it must be vitally important to everyone involved. This is why set-ups and payoffs for each character have to be crafted carefully and tracked throughout. I don't know why, but *Pretty Woman* comes to mind as a good example of this. Everybody arcs in *Pretty Woman*. Richard Gere, Julia Roberts, Laura San Giacomo — even the mentor figure, Hector Elizondo — are touched by the experience of this love story and transformed because of it. Everyone but the bad guy, Jason Alexander, who learns exactly zero.

Pretty Woman is one of hundreds of carefully crafted, successful movies in which this rule applies. All the really good movies do this, ones that you remember, that make you laugh *and* cry — the ones that you want to see a second time.

Hint, hint.

In a sense, stories are *about* change. And the measuring stick that tells us who succeeds and who doesn't is seen in the ability *to* change. Good guys are those who willingly accept change and see it as a positive force. Bad guys are those who refuse to change, who will curl up and die in their own juices, unable to move out of the rut their lives represent. To succeed in life is to be able to transform. That's why it's the basis not only of good storytelling but also the world's best-known religions. Change is good because it represents re-birth, the promise of a fresh start.

The Covenant of the Arc.

And don't we all want to believe that?

Don't we all want to jump into the swim of life after seeing a good movie? Don't we want to get out of our ruts, try something new, and be open to the healing power of change after experiencing a movie in which everybody arcs?

Yes, we do.

"Everybody arcs." That's one of the slogans I have written on a yellow Post-it® note and have stuck to the top of my iMac computer whenever I am writing a screenplay. And before I sit down to write, I make notes on how all my characters are going to arc by charting their stories as they are laid out on The Board, with the milestones of change noted as each character progresses through the story.

It is a must that you do the same.

If your script feels flat, if you are getting the sense that something's not happening in the story, do a quick Covenant of the Arc check and see if you need to do more work on making everybody change and grow and transform.

Everyone, that is, except the bad guy.

KEEP THE PRESS OUT!

Here's where I get to show off. Big time! You see, I learned this next lesson from Steven Spielberg. Personally. *Oh yeah... We worked together.* And it was one of the most educational experiences of my career. But in terms of the Immutable Laws of Screenwriting, that's the guy who really should write the book. I can only paraphrase.

To wit:

Keep the Press Out, the rule I learned from Steven Spielberg, was taught to me while we were developing a screenplay Jim Haggin and I had sold to Amblin called *Nuclear Family*. The premise of this movie is: A family camps out one night on a nuclear dumpsite and wakes up the next day with super powers. *Nuclear Family* is a wish-fulfillment comedy. Each family member has a need that their super-power quenches: Dad, an ad exec, gets the power to read minds and thus leaps ahead of his ratfink nemesis at work; Mom, a housewife, gets the power of telekinesis and becomes a super Mom who can move objects with her mind; Teen Son becomes The Flash and is suddenly his high school's star halfback; and Teen Daughter, forever behind in her schoolwork, gets a super brain and is now able to ace her SATs. It's a fun, special effects-laden fantasy — but it has a message, too. In the end, each of them gives up their powers. Being "successful" they find is not as important as being a family.

And yet, in the development process, we wanted to explore every option. When one of us, me I think, foolishly pitched that maybe we should have these powers discovered by the media, and to have the family swarmed by the news networks, Steven Spielberg said no, and he told us why.

You'll notice that there are no news crews in *E.T.*, the story of an extra-terrestrial creature who comes to Earth and into the lives of a similar cul de sac-dwelling family. Sure, you've got a really good reason for a news crew. They've caught one — a real live alien! And it's right there for everyone to see. But in rewrites with the screenwriter, Melissa Mathison, Spielberg discovered that it blew the reality of the premise to invite the press in. By keeping it contained among the family and on the block, by essentially keeping this secret between them and us, the audience, the magic stayed real. When you think about it, to bring the press into *E.T.* would indeed have ruined it. The term **breaking the fourth wall** springs to mind. That is the phrase that means violating the gossamer beneath the proscenium arch that separates the play from the audience. To bring the press into our little drama would have done the same.

Of course this is what separates the Spielbergs from the rest of us — including the Shyamalans. Keep the Press Out is a rule you won't see violated in any DreamWorks film, but in M. Night Shyamalan's *Signs* (there's that darn movie again) the rule is violated and, I think, suffers because of it.

Holed up in their Pennsylvania farmhouse, Mel Gibson's family is besieged by aliens. First the crop circles, then aliens arrive and try to break into Mel's house (and do what? We're not sure) *Night Of the Living Dead*-like. So while we're waiting for the attack, Mel and his family put on their tin-foil hats (Gad! What a movie!) and watch TV. There on CNN, news of other aliens landing all over the world is reported. There's even some spooky footage of one such alien invading a children's birthday party in South America.

And all that's interesting, but so what? What does it have to do with the drama of Mel trying to protect his family from the aliens that are swarming his house? I think it even makes their situation *less* desperate: They're no longer alone with this problem, *everyone's* dealing with it. Like in the *E.T.* example, bringing the press into "our secret" wrecks it. And it took me, as an audience member, out of the story.

The point is, bring the press in with care. Unless it's about the press, unless your movie involves a worldwide problem and we follow stories with characters all over the world, and it's important for them all to know about each other, take a tip from me... and Steven Spielberg:

Keep the Press Out.

SUMMARY

So now you know some basics and if you're like me, you want to know more and make up others as you go on. These are little Eurekas! that one experiences after watching a truckload of movies over the years. Suddenly you realize why things are done, what that scene *really* was for, and it makes you feel like a genius. Suddenly you're in on the tricks of screenwriting and have the experience of actually opening up the back of the Swiss watch, and seeing how the gears are put together. So THAT'S how that works! you suddenly think.

You feel like you're learning the magician's secrets.

Once you see these little tricks, the urge to put a label to them can't be far behind. This is why Save the Cat, the Pope in the Pool, Black Vet, and Keep the Press Out are memorable — to me anyway — and vital to be so. Yes, it's good, slangy fun. It's also a way not to forget what you've learned. And when you catch yourself drifting into a mistake, or pushing up against a rule you'd like to break, these pithy little lessons give you an instant assessment on the pros and cons of minding or breaking... The Law. How many times have I caught myself drifting into one or more of these errors during the course of creating and writing a screenplay? Well, many. But the point of all this is to learn shortcuts to save time.

Screenwriting is like solving a puzzle over and over. You get faster with practice. The more stories you break, the more outlines you beat out to their completion, the more screenplays you tag with THE END, the better you get. These shortcuts are essential time-savers.

EXERCISES

1. Name a movie hero that is unlikable. Did the creators of the movie do anything to deal with this? What new Save the Cat tricks can be used to make a hero likable, but not so phony-baloney that we reject the device?

2. Find examples in other movies that use the Pope in the Pool. Does burying the exposition hurt or enhance your understanding of what's going on in the plot?

3. Fix *Spider-Man*. Let's say you don't have to follow the storyline that was created in the Marvel comic book Stan Lee created. What changes would you make to the screenplay that could eliminate its Double Mumbo Jumbo?

4. Since you liked M. Night Shyamalan's *Signs* and think that I am out of my mind for not liking it, e-mail me at the address found at the end of Chapter One and explain M. Night Shyamalan's *Unbreakable* to me — a movie so preposterous it makes *Signs* look like *Battleship Potemkin*. But remember, I've been working on my argument and am still ticked about not getting my $10 back from the theater!

7 WHAT'S WRONG WITH THIS PICTURE?

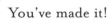

You've made it!

Congratulations!

You've followed my advice, you've done the prep, you've hit your marks like a pro, and you've finally written THE END.

And whether you've got 90 pages or 130, you've accomplished what you set out to do: You've written a draft of a movie.

You are amazing!

So before going on any further, let's bask for a moment in the glory of your success.

Finishing a screenplay separates you from five out of 10 would-be screenwriters who only talk about writing their movie ideas. You have increased your odds of success immeasurably by doing the work. And whether it's your first script or your twenty-first, you have one more notch on your belt in a never-ending shootout with your creative demons. You've not only written a screenplay, you've gotten better at the job, and each one you write makes you better still.

Me? I've written or co-written 75 screenplays, including TV scripts, and when I compare the ones I wrote initially to the ones I'm writing now, I can see real growth in my skills. I can always get better at this. And as long as I maintain the attitude that the next script will be my best yet, and keep being excited about the process, I know I can't fail.

But back to you. You've finished! And yet even though you're a proud parent, you're starting to have a few nagging doubts about this creation of yours. Some parts of your script don't work, you know that. And some parts, you think secretly, might be a train wreck. But having put your script aside for about a week, which I recommend (longer if you can stand it), you now come back to that glorious hatchling, read it over from start to finish... and are suddenly struck dumb.

It's awful!!!

Characters are flat! Nothing happens or happens so slowly you can't believe a human being wrote it and not some mental patient. What were you thinking? You're not *done*! You haven't even started! What's worse, now that you know the awful truth, now that you realize how bad you are at this, you don't even want to keep going. You've gone from the high of mountaintop megalomania to the depths of self-loathing.

Am I getting the basic roller-coaster ride?

Well, fear not. It always happens. You've got a ways to go. But before you jump off the Hollywood sign, take a breath. There's a way to prop up this puppy again and get you back on your mega-lomaniac way.

I can help you pinpoint and fix some of your rough spots.

And it's really not all that hard.

It's just a matter of being honest in your assessment and willing to do the work to fix all the problems. So, here are typical trouble spots that others have faced, long before you came along, that may help in your rewrite.

THE HERO LEADS

A common mistake in a lot of rough drafts is the problem of the **inactive hero**. It's often hard to spot, especially if you've done everything else right. You've gone out of your way to thoroughly plot your screenplay; every beat moves the story forward. But somehow you forgot to inform your lead.

Your hero is being *dragged* through the story, showing up when he's supposed to but for no reason. Your hero seems unmotivated, his goal vague, the driving force that should be guiding him is MIA. Imagine what it would be like if a detective in a murder mystery acted this way. We'll call him Johnny Entropy because he's an existential layabout who has no motivation and can't be paid to care. Johnny shows up, he goes through the motions of the case but he doesn't want to. He never seeks clues, they're just given to him. He has no goals. He exists but he doesn't know why. Johnny's motto is: "What's the point? We're all gonna die some day anyway."

Does this describe your hero?

Well if so, you've got to fix it, because if there's one thing we know for sure it's the truism that: *The hero must be proactive*. It's The Law. If he's not, he's not a hero.

Here's a checklist to see if your lead needs more oomph:

1. **Is your hero's goal clearly stated in the set-up?** Is what your hero wants obvious to you and to the audience? If not, or if you don't know what your hero's goal is, figure it out. And make sure that goal is spoken aloud and restated in action and words throughout the story.

2. **Do clues of what to do next just come to your hero or does he seek them out?** If it all happens too easily for your hero, something's wrong. Your hero cannot be handed his destiny, he must work for it at every step.

3. **Is your hero active or passive?** If the latter, you have a problem. Everything your hero does has to spring from his burning desire and his deeply held need to achieve his goal. If he can't be bothered, or can get to that burning desire mañana, you've got *Hamlet* — fine if you're Shakespeare, bad if you're writing for Vin Diesel.

4. **Do other characters tell your hero what to do or does he tell them?** Here's a great rule of thumb: A hero never asks questions! The hero knows and others around him look to *him* for answers, not the other way around. If you see a lot of question marks in your hero's dialogue, there's a problem. The hero knows; he never asks.

My guess is that if any of the above rings true, you have an inactive hero on your hands. And scripts with inactive heroes lay there like a lox. So fix it! Give your hero a little kick in the butt and tell him to get in the game. Come on, let's see some leadership! That's what heroes do.

TALKING THE PLOT

Another problem found in poorly executed screenplays is "talking the plot," and it's a dead giveaway that the writer is green. Characters will walk into scenes and say, "Well, you're my sister, you should know!" and "This sure isn't like the time I was the star fullback for the N.Y. Giants until my... accident." This kind of dialogue is... (say it with me) *bad!* And yet I completely understand why it's in there.

You have backstory and plot to explain, and there's no way to say it, so you resort to having your characters say it for you. And it sucks. It's one of those Guaranteed-to-Have-Your-Script-Thrown-Across-the-Room-by-the-Reader things.

The reason it makes the hair on the back of our necks stand up is that it's unreal. Who talks like that? You've forgotten that your characters don't serve you, they serve themselves. They should walk into each scene with their own goals and say what's on their minds, not yours. You must reveal who they are and what they want, their hopes, dreams, and fears, by *how* they say it as much as *what* they say. Good dialogue tells us more about what's going on in its **subtext** than on its surface. Subtle is better. And talking the plot is like using a sledgehammer. It's overkill.

An adjunct to this rule of bad dialogue is "Show, Don't Tell," another of the most frequent mistakes found in newbie screenplays. You can say more about a relationship in trouble by seeing a husband eye a pretty young thing as he and his wife are walking down the street than by three pages of dialogue about how their marriage counseling sessions are going. Movies are stories told in pictures. So why would you resort to telling us when you can show us? It's so much more economical! You want to make sure the audience knows about a guy's N.Y. Giants past? Show team pictures on the wall of his apartment, give him a limp (from the accident that ended his career, but only if it's germane), sneak it in with subtle references. Want to make sure we know a fight has occurred between two people? Have them talk about anything *but* the fight. If handled right, the audience will get it. They're a lot more perceptive than you think.

By showing and not telling, you leave room for your characters to be at their best — that's being active, with their own separate agendas for being there, not yours.

The truth is that movies are so much about what happens that we must learn about characters by what they do, not by what they say. As in Life, character is revealed by action taken, not by words spoken. And in a good movie, information doesn't come out in dialogue, it comes out in the verve and forward motion of the story. You must get out all your wonderful plot and backstory on the fly, or better yet, not at all. You should be more concerned with what's happening now than what happened before the story started. So when you feel yourself drifting into talking the plot, don't. And when you think you're talking too much: Show, don't tell.

MAKE THE BAD GUY BADDER

An addition to the idea that The Hero Leads is the rule that says: The bad guy must be as bad as possible. Many times, your hero will do everything he's supposed to. He'll be proactive; he'll seek out and overcome obstacles; he'll do amazing things — and still we're unimpressed. He's such a nobody! He's so average, so unheroic, so insignificant! We don't want to see nobodies onscreen, we want to see heroes.

If this seems familiar, then maybe it's not the hero but his antagonist that's the problem, and there's an easy solution. Maybe you need to make the bad guy... badder!

This is a common first-draft problem. I think it's because we want our hero to win so badly that we don't want to make it impossible for him to do so. But we cannot protect our hero from danger and challenge; we must throw a little more at him than he is able to take. And making the bad guy badder automatically makes the hero bigger. It's one of those Immutable Laws of Screenwriting.

Think about James Bond. What makes James Bond a super spy isn't the gadgets or the girls or the car. What makes him James Bond is Goldfinger, Blofeld, and Dr. No. How dull would 007 be if his enemy was an evil accountant who was juggling the books down at the local bank. Where would the challenge be in that? Suddenly the gadgets and the car and the charm aren't necessary. James can just do a quick skip-trace on the Internet and be done in time for Martini Hour. He needs someone bigger to play with to make his own heroism bigger. He needs an antagonist whose powers match his own.

In many a well-told movie, the hero and the bad guy are very often two halves of the same person struggling for supremacy, and for that reason are almost equal in power and ability. How many movies can you name that have a hero and a bad guy who are two halves of the same persona? Think about *Batman* (Michael Keaton and Jack Nicholson), *Die Hard* (Bruce Willis and Alan Rickman), and even *Pretty Woman* (Richard Gere and Jason Alexander). Aren't the hero and the bad guy of each of these movies the light and dark sides of the same person? Aren't they the positive and negative x-ray of one soul? And each has something the other wants — even if it's just an answer to what makes them the way they are.

The point is that the hero and the bad guy are a matched set and should be of equal skill and strength, with the bad guy being just slightly more powerful than the hero because he is willing to go to any lengths to win. After all, the bad guy has given up on having "family values" by definition. This does not mean you make the bad guy impossible to beat — just a challenge that *looks* impossible. So if your hero and your bad guy are not of equal strength, make them so, but give the edge to the bad guy. By ratcheting up the power and invincibility of the bad guy, the hero will have to do more that we can admire. Making the bad guy just out of reach of the ability of the hero to defeat him elevates our hero.

TURN, TURN, TURN

This is another of those slogans that I have written on a faded Post-it® note. It's been stuck above my desk for 20 years. It was the first piece of wisdom I ever heard about screenwriting and I'll be damned if I know who told me.

But this anonymous advisor has guided me ever since.

The basis of the "Turn, Turn, Turn" rule is: The plot doesn't just move ahead, it spins and intensifies as it goes. It is the difference between velocity (a constant speed) and acceleration (an increasing speed). And the rule is: It's not enough for the plot to go forward, it must go forward faster, and with more complexity, to the climax.

If things happen in your movie but aren't interesting, then all you've got is a chase. They go here, they go there, but nothing about the chase provokes any activity behind the audience's eye-balls. We're just watching stuff happen, but nothing about it is engaging or humanly compelling.

And that's... (Anybody? Anybody?)... bad. Right.

Let's take, for example, a very loud and busy movie, *The Cat in the Hat*, starring Mike Meyers. Apart from the fact that it's one of the more inappropriate kids' movies ever made, it's a great example of lots of STUFF! happening, all over the place, TONS! of action... without anything *happening* at all. It's kinetic eye candy with no forward motion. It's a CHASE! with no stakes. They go here, they go there, but I don't give a damn and don't know why I'm watching. It proves the point that you can have lots of action and still not have a story. It moves forward, but there's no Turn, Turn, Turn.

More must be revealed along every step of the plot about your characters and what all this action means. To that end, you, the writer of this plot, must show how it affects your characters as you go along. You must show flaws, reveal treacheries, doubts, and fears *of* the heroes — and threats *to* them. You must expose hidden powers, untapped resources, and dark motivations for the bad guys that the hero doesn't know about. Show facets of that spinning diamond of plot, let the reflected light amaze the audience. The diamond cannot merely move across the screen, it must Turn, Turn, Turn in order to truly dazzle us. Show us all of it. Let the light play off its many sides; let's see some of that detail!

The same goes for the speed of the plot. As the grip of the bad guy tightens around the hero, things happen faster, and the pressure exerted in the vice-like grip of the forces opposing the hero will finally explode in its Act Three climax with a rush of energy and emotion. If you don't feel your plot intensifying as you make the midpoint turn and start heading for the finish, you have problems.

Turn, Turn, Turn reminds us to accelerate and reveal all with verve as we move the plot forward. Turn, Turn, Turn tells us to make the plot more dynamic and less inert.

So if your screenplay's plot feels in any way static or flat, try looking at it from its other angles. And make it accelerate, not just move forward. Make it Turn, Turn, Turn.

THE EMOTIONAL COLOR WHEEL

When they say a good movie is "like a roller-coaster ride," they mean that as an audience member watching the story unfold, your emotions have been wrung out. You've laughed; you've cried; you've been aroused; you've been scared; you've felt regret, anger, frustration, near-miss anxiety and, ultimately, breathtaking triumph. And when the lights come up, you walk out of the theater feeling absolutely drained.

Whew! What a movie!

Whether it's a comedy or a drama, wringing out the emotions of the audience is the name of the game. Making it an emotional experience, using *all* the emotions, is what it's about. Think why that is. We go to the movies not only to escape reality, and to ultimately learn a little lesson about Life, but to experience a dream state where Life and its attendant emotions are recreated in a safe environment. Like a good dream, we must live the movie; we must run in place along with the hero in our sleep, clutch our pillows at the love scene, and hide under the covers during the breathtaking climax of the film to wake exhausted but fulfilled, wrung out, worked out, and satisfied.

So your movie doesn't have this, so what? So it's one-note emotionally? If it's a comedy and it's funny all the way through, what's the problem? If it's a drama and it's tense from start to finish, that's all. What's wrong with that?

Well, let's take a look at two filmmakers I never thought I'd reference in any how-to book: the Farrelly Brothers. They write and direct comedies like *Something About Mary*, *Shallow Hal*, and *Stuck On You*, and are known for hilarious, ribald set pieces. But if you think all they are is funny, you're wrong. These guys work it emotionally. In each of their movies they have scenes of great fear, scenes of intense longing, scenes of lust, scenes of human foible. Their movies work because they use every color in the emotional color wheel. It's not just one-note funny.

And you can do the same.

If your script feels one-note emotionally, go back and flesh it out using all the colors in the palette. Where is your lust scene? Where is your frustration scene? Where is your scary scene? And if you don't have these, take a scene that's just funny or just dramatic and try to play it for one of the missing colors. A good way to do this is to actually choose a color of each of the missing emotions and go back and tag certain scenes to change the emotional tone from one type to another. Take those scenes and use the same action, the same +/-, the same conflict and result, but play it for lust instead of laughs, jealousy instead of flat-out, stare-down dramatic conflict. By varying the emotions you use, you'll create a much more rewarding experience for everyone.

Don't believe me? Go and look at any Farrelly Brothers movie.

"HI HOW ARE YOU I'M FINE"

Flat dialogue even happens to good movies. But your script will never be a movie if you have dull, lifeless repartee. And when you find yourself reading page after page of this "place-holder" talk, you know you're in trouble.

You're bored!

And that is...(Wait for it)... *bad*. Absolutely.

"Hi how are you I'm fine" tells us just how boring flat dialogue can be and what a waste of space it is. Flat dialogue is the kind that anyone can say. And odds are that if your script if full of lines that are right out of real life, that ring true but ring dull, you're not working hard enough to make the characters come to life. Because odds are that if your dialogue is flat, so are the people speaking it.

Engaging characters talk differently than you and I. They have a way of saying things, even the most mundane things, which raise them above the norm. A character's dialogue is your opportunity to *reveal* character and tell us who this person is as much as what he is saying. How someone talks *is* character and can highlight all manner of that character's past, inner demons, and outlook on life.

Every time a character speaks is your chance to show that.

If you don't think you have flat dialogue, try a simple trick I learned from Mike Cheda. After reading one of my early scripts, he broke the news to me: "Your characters all talk the same." Well, naturally I was insulted; I was ticked. And young bullhead that I was, I did not believe Mike Cheda. What did *he* know?!

Then Mike showed me this simple Bad Dialogue Test: Take a page of your script and cover up the names of the people speaking. Now read the repartee as it goes back and forth between two or more characters. Can you tell who is speaking without seeing the name above the dialogue? The first time I tried it, there in Mike's office at Barry & Enright, I was stunned. Damn it, he was right. I couldn't tell one of my characters from the others, and then and there I figured out something else too: All the characters had MY voice!! In a good script, *every* character must speak differently. Every character must have a unique way of saying even the most mundane "Hi How are you I'm fine" kind of chat.

My best learning experience in this regard was an early draft of a script called *Big, Ugly Baby!*, an alien-switched-at-birth comedy. I gave *every* character a verbal tic. One stuttered, one did malapropisms, one was an Okie versed in Sartre, and the Alien parents (my favorite characters) always yelled, a point I reinforced by having at least one word in every sentence they spoke CAPITALIZED! While you don't have to be this drastic in your script, that exercise showed me how I could make characters richer. (And more fun to read out loud, btw.) I had learned that amping up even the most "Hi how are you I'm fine" kind of dialogue revealed everything about each of my characters and made the read 100% better.

TAKE A STEP BACK

I have just been involved in 10 months of rewrites. My partner Sheldon and I were working on our Golden Fleece and it took seven — count 'em seven — drafts to get it right. One of the reasons it took so long is that we had made a basic mistake. We had broken the rule of "Take a Step Back." Just so you know, it happens to everybody — even the pros.

As mentioned in Chapter Four, our story is about a kid who is kicked out of military school and sent home only to find that his parents have moved away without telling him. So our kid hero goes on the road and has lots of fun adventures where he interacts with people and helps them, because he's a good kid who causes flowers to bloom and changes the lives of strangers wherever he goes. Our mistake was that the way we had created the character — a nice kid who helps others — didn't give him anywhere to go. Our hero had already changed. He didn't need this journey. He was the same person he was at the beginning that he was at the end. And the fixing of that problem, draft by draft, took forever. Each draft was about taking him back a step emotionally so the journey means something. *Okay, a little bit further, okay let's take him all the way back!* It seems easy now, but in the middle of it, we couldn't figure it out. We couldn't see that what we needed to do was take our hero back as far as possible, so that the story would be about his growth. And believe it or not, this kind of mistake happens all the time.

A lot of us know where our heroes end up and don't want to put them through the torment of growth, so we avoid the pain for them. And just like raising a child, you can't do that. These characters have to grow by getting bumped on the nose, and whether we like it or not, we have to let them. In our case, Sheldon and I liked our hero so much and wanted him to come out in the end being upbeat, positive, and special — but we didn't want to see his struggle to become that. It was like reading the answers at the back of the book without doing the work on the test questions. We wanted to get there so badly, we didn't see that getting there *was* the story. And showing the bumps along the way made the pay-off greater.

Take a Step Back applies to all your characters. In order to show how everyone grows and changes in the course of your story, you must take them all back to the starting point. Don't get caught up in the end result and deny us the fun of how they get there. We want to see it happen. To everyone.

This is just one more example of how movies must show the audience everything: all the change, all the growth, all the action of a hero's journey. By taking it all back as far as possible, by drawing the bow back to its very quivering end point, the flight of the arrow is its strongest, longest, and best. The Take a Step Back rule double-checks this.

If you feel like your story or any of its characters isn't showing us the entire flight, the entire journey… Take a Step Back and show it all to us. We want to see it.

A LIMP AND AN EYE PATCH

Sometimes in a screenplay, the basics are done, your hero and bad guy are great, the plot explodes and intensifies after the midpoint, and everybody's got snappy dialogue. Everything's great except for one small problem: There seem to be too many minor characters. It's hard to tell one from another. Readers will confuse that guy with this other guy. And it bugs you! Isn't it obvious?!

What has happened is that you have not given us a hook to hang our hats on for each of the characters that are vital to your story. And while we often rationalize this by saying "Oh well, they'll handle that in casting!" I've got one word for you: Ha! You won't see casting if your reader can't see characters. But there's an easy way to solve this:

Make sure every character has "A Limp and an Eyepatch."

Every character has to have a unique way of speaking, but also something memorable that will stick him in the reader's mind. The reader has to have a visual clue, often a running visual reminder, which makes remembering a character easier. A Limp and an Eyepatch may seem like a silly way to think about how to attach traits to characters to make sure we remember them, but it works — if you remember to do it.

Often the realization that you need something like this comes from a reader. A great example of A Limp and an Eyepatch happened to me and shows just how amazing this simple device can be. Sheldon and I were writing our ill-fated *Really Mean Girls*. We had one character, the lead boy, who has a crush on our lead girl and acts as the "Speaker of Truth" whenever he is around, keeping the lead girl on the straight and narrow with his moral compass. He's a funny kid, mature beyond his years, the type who will be a sterling adult but right now is "too smart for his own good." He was vital to the plot, but somehow unmemorable on the page. Our manager, Andy Cohen, read draft after draft and kept getting stuck on the boy. Who was he? Yes, he had an important function, but why was he interesting? We tried changing dialogue, making him funnier, smarter, but still got the same note.

Finally, Sheldon came up with a brilliant fix. When we meet the boy for the first time, we described him as wearing a black t-shirt and sporting a wispy soul-patch on his chin. Emblematically it fit, showing his yearning to be hip and older on the inside and not quite cutting it in his appearance. And every time he appeared we referenced this. We gave the script back to Andy, and he called us to say he didn't know what we'd done but the character of the boy really popped for him now. The boy jumped off the page and registered in his mind. We had done very little overall, he was the same kid, we just gave him A Limp and an Eyepatch.

And it made all the difference.

Is this technique "fake" or "artifice"? No, it's screenwriting. It's the job. So when you find yourself with one or several unidentifiable characters who are getting lost in the shuffle, try saying what I say now all the time:

I think this guy needs A Limp and an Eyepatch.

IS IT PRIMAL?

I have used the term "primal" throughout this book. To me it is my touchstone both in creating a script and fixing it once it's done. "Is it primal?" is a question I ask from the beginning to the end of a project, and making it more primal is the name of the game. To ask "Is It Primal?" or "Would a Caveman Understand?" is to ask if you are connecting with the audience at a basic level. Does your plot hinge on primal drives like survival, hunger, sex, protection of loved ones, or fear of death? At the root of anyone's goal in a movie must be something that basic, even if on its surface it seems to be about something else. By making what drives your characters more primal, you'll not only ground everything that happens in principles that connect in a visceral way, you also make it easier to sell your story all over the world.

Think about it.

Everyone in China "gets" a love story. Everyone in South America understands a *Jaws* or an *Alien* because "Don't Get Eaten" is primal — even without snappy dialogue.

But this can also go for little fixes of minor characters or subplots in a script that's not working. Are these characters motivated by primal drives? It's another way of saying: Are these characters acting like recognizable human beings? At their core, they must be. Or else you are not addressing primal issues.

Let's say you have a high-falutin' concept: stockbrokers rigging the international bond market. Fine. All very interesting. But at its core, no matter what the plot is, by making each character's desire more primal, that plot is grounded in a reality that everyone can understand — suddenly it's not about stockbrokers, it's about human beings trying to survive.

Here are primal drives in the storylines of a few hit films:

> The desire to save one's family (*Die Hard*)
> The desire to protect one's home (*Home Alone*)
> The desire to find a mate (*Sleepless in Seattle*)
> The desire to exact revenge (*Gladiator*)
> The desire to survive (*Titanic*)

Each of these is about a primal need that might be better seen as a biological need, the prime directive. The desire to win the lottery is, in fact, the desire to have more food, more wives, make more children, to be able to reproduce at will. The desire for revenge is, in fact, the desire to knock off a competing DNA carrier and propel your own DNA forward. The desire to find one's parent or child is the desire to shore up and defend existing DNA and survive.

You may think your story is about something more "sophisticated" than this; it's not. At its core it must be about something that resonates at a caveman level.

All together now: When in doubt ask, "Is It Primal?"

SUMMARY

So now you've seen how you can double-check your work using simple rules of the road. If your script feels flat or if you get back comments from readers who can't quite put their finger on it, but know something's wrong, here are seven easy thought-starters to help you find the weak spot.

And fix it.

Ask yourself these questions, the "Is It Broken?" Test:

1. Does my hero lead the action? Is he proactive at every stage of the game and fired up by a desire or a goal?

2. Do my characters "talk the plot"? Am I saying things a novelist would say through my characters instead of letting it be seen in the action of my screenplay?

3. Is the bad guy bad enough? Does he offer my hero the right kind of challenge? Do they both belong in this movie?

4. Does my plot move faster and grow more intense after the midpoint? Is more revealed about the hero and the bad guy as we come in to the Act Three finale?

5. Is my script one-note emotionally? Is it all drama? All comedy? All sadness? All frustration? Does it feel like it needs, but does not offer, emotion breaks?

6. Is my dialogue flat? After doing the Bad Dialogue Test does it seem like everyone talks the same? Can I tell one character from another just by how he or she speaks?

7. Do my minor characters stand out from each other, and are they easy to differentiate by how they look in the mind's eye? Is each unique in speech, look, and manner?

8. Does the hero's journey start as far back as it can go? Am I seeing the entire length of the emotional growth of the hero in this story?

9. Is it primal? Are my characters, at their core, reaching out for a primal desire — to be loved, to survive, to protect family, to exact revenge?

If you are having any nagging doubts about any of the above, you now know what to do. You have the tools to go back in and fix it. But will you? That's the rub. Here's a tip: When in doubt, do it. Odds are that if you, or your initial batch of readers, have found problems with your screenplay, everyone else will too. Don't be lazy! Don't say "Oh well, no one will notice" because... they will. It is better to be brilliant now and have the guts to fix your mistakes before your script's sitting on Steven Spielberg's desk.

You only get the one shot at a first impression. Try to get over the love affair you have with yourself and your work (God knows I've been in love with my own a thousand times!!) and do what needs to be done. This is what separates the pros from the wannabes — that nagging voice that says: "It sucks!" And the mature, adult, professional voice that quickly chimes in: "And I know how to fix it!"

EXERCISES

1. Go back over your list of movies in your favorite genre, pick one that feels weak, and use the Is It Broken? Test to see if it can be improved.

2. Take another of your favorite movies from your genre and examine the hero/bad guy relationship. Imagine torquing this relationship out of whack by making the bad guy less powerful or ordinary. Does this simple change make the hero less interesting too?

3. Try "talking the plot" in real life. Seriously. Go to a party or meet with a group of friends and say: "I sure am glad I'm a screenwriter who was born in Chicago!" or "Gosh, you've been my friend for 20 years ever since we met in High School!" See what reaction you get to this kind of dialogue.

8 FINAL FADE IN

And so we come to the end of our screenwriting confab.

We've discussed many relevant topics and while I've been writing this book, and working on screenplays of my own thank you very much, a lot has happened out here in Hollywoodland:

> Sequels have met with mixed success.

> Many pre-sold franchises did well but some died miserable deaths.

> The open-huge-in—the-first-week strategy (3,000+ theaters) even-if-you-drop-70%-80%-in-the-second-week of a film's release still recouped a majority of most films' budgets, assuring this tactic will continue.

> And family films outperformed every other type of movie, a truism that was met with the resounding sound of... crickets... by the Zegna-suited slicksters. (It's hard to be cool at the cocktail party when you make — ugh! — PG flicks.)

In short, it's more than interesting; it's a boom time, a gold rush. And the most important thing for you to know is that it's still a highly profitable business with lots of reason to invest in new talent. So here is the good news and bad news as it relates to your spec screenplay.

The good news is: The studios have money to buy your script. And the lack of stellar success in the pre-sold franchise arena should indicate they need you. More than ever they must have original ideas. So buying your spec makes sense.

The bad news is: They attribute all their success to themselves. Shrewder marketing, better accounting, more control over how ideas get turned into movies — that's how they did it, ladies and gentlemen! God love 'em! Studio executives keep praying for the sun to rise and each dawn assume it was their prayers that made it happen.

But this should not deter you. If you have gotten anything out of this book, it's that selling a script has a lot more to do with thinking of your screenplay as a "business plan" than ever before. If you have a creative approach, you too can sell to Hollywood. And if you do, you have a bright future. A catchy logline and a killer title will get you noticed. A well-structured screenplay will keep you in the game, and knowing how to fix your script — and any other script you may be presented with — will get you a career. If you have mastered the demands of the job as outlined in this book, you will win at this game.

But we are getting ahead of ourselves?

How, you may ask, do you even get in the door?!

AMBITION VS. FATE

Before the first class is over, invariably I will be asked the one burning question on every screenwriter's mind:

"How do I get an agent?"

Would you believe me if I told you that it's all luck? Would you call me crazy if I advised you not to worry about it, that it will happen when it happens? Probably not. But that may be because I am very comfortable with the subject of how to sell myself. I personally love the business of marketing my scripts and me. I am not afraid to pick up the phone, meet someone at a party, and actually call them the next day (if they give me their card) or finagle friends to get me introductions to people I think would like to meet me.

I think I have something to offer. I like the business and I like meeting the people in it. And the worst thing that can happen, I figure, is that someone will say "no."

So here are two stories about how I got my first agents. One is a demonstration of ambition, one an example of fate.

I got my first agent by sheer pluck. My friends and I had written and produced a TV pilot called *The Blank Show*. A funny parody of what was then the brand-new phenomenon of cable TV, we had made it on a shoestring and once we were done with it, we didn't know what to do. I volunteered to market it myself. I came to Los Angeles, submitted it to Public Access TV, and got a commitment for a day and time it would air. Then for weeks I plastered the westside (where I assumed producers lived) with fliers telling the day and time our show would be on. It finally ran one Sunday night and, sure enough, the next day, Monday morning, I got a call from the producing partner of Budd Friedman, owner of the

Improv. He loved our show! Would my friends and I be interested in being represented? I arranged to have my gang of cohorts come to Los Angeles for a meeting with Budd, who offered to manage us there and then. A little luck and ambition had gotten us noticed. And while our comedy troupe eventually broke up, I have maintained my friendship with Budd Friedman to this day.

That's what "working it" can do, so you should always be working it. But here's where fate is better.

My next agent, and the best one I ever had, I met through circumstances that were much more serendipitous. On a break from my duties as a Production Assistant for a sitcom called *Teachers Only* at NBC, I decided to go home to Santa Barbara for the weekend. And even though I was tired from the drive, I was restless. I decided to go to a local club to get a drink and hopefully meet girls. And I did. I met a girl I was smitten with on sight, and who eventually became my girlfriend. No, she wasn't an agent. But her best friend wanted to be one. I hit it off with her, too. And when she was promoted to agent at Writers & Artists, I was one of the first people she asked to be her client. I immediately said yes.

And that's how I came to be represented by Hilary Wayne. All because I stopped in to have a drink at a bar.

Hilary and I went on to have a fabulous relationship. She was the best agent I ever had. She made great deals for me, understood my writing and my ability to conceptualize, and she formed the foundation of my entire career. Though she herself was new to the game, she had a real knack not just for selling but also for positioning both script and writer in the marketplace. Hilary knew how to build careers and she built mine from scratch. Our relationship coincided with that point in Hollywood history when the "spec sale" was king. This was a time when studio heads would knock themselves out to take a virgin script away from another studio; they'd bid the price up into the millions to do so. And Hilary was a master at setting up these grudge matches, pitting executive against executive, and engineering sales that became the headline on next day's front page of *Variety*.

What I had found in Hilary was not just an agent, but a partner. What made it work was that we were on the same wavelength; we were both hungry to succeed, and went out of our way to respect the marketplace and deliver to it what we thought it needed. We read the tea leaves, I went back and made product, and she sold the product. And we made millions of dollars doing it. Hilary passed away in 1998 or I would still be working with her. And I often wonder what she would make of the business today. The landscape has changed and the spec sale fever is no longer what it was, but Hollywood still needs good ideas and good writers. No matter how you find your way in this maze, you must be bold. And you must find your own Hilary Wayne because you can't do it alone.

It's one thing for me to tell you my tales, it's another to ask what I would do if I were starting out again or if I wanted to find new representation and sell myself from scratch today. I am lucky — I don't mind getting out from behind my computer and meeting people. Not every one of you is like that. As writers we tend to be insular, introverted, and introspective. But if you want to sell your script, you have to sell yourself — and I say this in the most healthy and positive sense. There is no crass salesmanship involved if you are genuinely interested in your subject. And if you seek out people to be partners in this game, whom you can help as much as they can help you, then it's mutually beneficial.

That's always been my attitude, anyway.

So maybe I can plant a few positive visualizations in your brain and you can see yourself following through on a few of them. Because being a talented screenwriter, and writing even the most perfect script, is only a small part of what will be needed to get you where you want to go. You will need to get out of your workroom and mingle. You will have to put on a clean shirt and shine your shoes and smile.

PREPARING THE FIELD

Like any well-plotted story with a (hopefully) happy ending, you must make a plan and follow it step by step.

Here's what you've got:

You've got you, a screenwriter with x number of scripts to your credit, varying degrees of success in selling them, and a great big crush on movies and moviemakers.

You've got your product — your best screenplay — and several pitches (even if they're for screenplays you've already written), and if you've followed the advice of Chapter One, your loglines and titles are killer — and ready to go.

You've even got a rough idea of what you need next: An agent who will help you sell these projects, and producers who will either buy them from you or go into partnership with you to get these projects set up, sold, and made into movies.

If you don't have that list, start making one:
> Go on the Internet and check out the Hollywood Creative Directory (*www.hcdonline.com*); if you feel like shelling out $50 or so, get a copy (you should). Read that thing and get to know it. Production companies, contact names, fellow writers, and producers with projects in your genre is the place to start.

> Likewise pick up a copy of the HCD Talent Agency directory and make a similar list. Include agents at big agencies and small, who like the same movies you like.

And now, you must start being really clever.

THAT SOUL-EATING FIRST CONTACT

You can contact anyone by letter, you can camp out on doorsteps and stalk your victims, you can produce *The Blank Show* and get it on L.A. Public Access and wait for the phone to ring, but whatever your method, slowly and surely, you must introduce you and your product to "them." In my opinion, making it about *you* first is the key. Making it personal, letting them meet and know *you*, is the best way to make the introduction to your work. My genius agent Hilary always said, and it should be on a plaque in the Hall of Fame: Every Sale Has a Story! The story is you. But how are you going to get that story told to the people on your list? Well:

> *In person* is better than a phone call...
> A *phone call* is better than a query letter...
> A *query letter* is better than an e-mail...
> And an *e-mail* (from a stranger) is usually when I push DELETE on my computer — unless I've been forewarned that it's coming or it can do something for me today.

The key to all of this is to not think so much about your immediate goals but your long-term ones. Sure you need an agent, right now! But you also need to build a reputation. If you are lucky enough to have a career, you will be bumping into these people again and again for years. So try not to burn any bridges, or at least try not to burn them all the way down. Be nice. Be considerate. Be helpful. Be upbeat.

But keep knocking on doors and showing your face.

Try to put yourself in the shoes of everyone you speak to. What is it that they want? How can you make dealing with you easier on them? And what are they going to get out of the interaction that will make meeting you worth their time?

One of the golden rules is it's easier to get an agent when you have a deal that needs closing. And it is also easier to pitch you if someone has already bought something from you. This is why I always recommend that if any legitimate entity wants to option your screenplay, even for little money, and no one else has offered you anything — grab it. I can't tell you the value of having someone go first. And having projects in process, no matter how minor in terms of money up front, tells others you don't have the plague. It also gives you something to talk about when you meet new people.

So now you know what you're selling and whom you want to sell to. But how can you make your proposal different? How can you catch the eye of someone who gets proposals all the time? Would you blanch if I told you it was just a matter of turning the crank again and again until something happens?

Because that's all it takes.

Just keep turning the crank. Any inroad, any one at all, is a gigantic leap forward. And while you may not get an agent right away, or make a sale right away, you are making progress every time you write a query letter, pick up the phone, or meet someone for coffee. Here are a few signs that you are making progress in marketing you:

> An agent or producer says your project is not for him, but to keep him in mind for future scripts.

> You talk to an agent or producer that *you* like. This is a sign, fellow pilgrims! It is just as important for you to feel chemistry with him as his feeling chemistry with you. You've identified someone you will want to get in touch with again, even if it's "no" now.

> You have whittled a list of 50 possibles down to three maybes. Those 47 no's had to be gotten through. Every no is one step closer to a yes. But by God you did the work! The yes is that much nearer.

> You get a referral. Everyone you contact must be asked this question at some point in the process of saying no: "Is there anyone else you can recommend that I contact about my career?" *Referrals are gold** and everyone I know is thrilled to oblige with one. Believe it or not, people want to help you succeed.

NETWORKING

When the agent and producer route has been thoroughly sifted through, where else can you go to get help? It *is* who you know, damn it. So how are you going to reach out? Well, these things can be done — even without an agent:

> **Film Festivals** — There's one in your town or somewhere close enough to attend. Go there. Get business cards, pitch your script, hear other pitches. A contact is a contact and every

---

*This is how I got hired as a page at NBC. I cold-called a producer for a job. I met with him, he had nothing for me, but the meeting went so well he called his friend at NBC and got me an interview. The producer had been a page himself.

person you meet knows 30 other people. Keep in touch post-festival and ask for referrals. Figure out how you can return the favor. Ask how you can help with *their* projects.

> **Classes** — Go where other screenwriters go, but also go where aspiring producers go. Near me at UCLA there's a Producer's Seminar every semester — what a great place for a writer to go to meet the next wave of young hotshot producers in town. The local university in your town probably has similar courses.

> **Screenwriting Groups** — There are lots of these online, as well as in local communities. And I belong to one of the best, a savvy little bunch of scribblers called The Screenplayers (*www.screenplayers.net*). These are bands of screenwriters pooling their resources to help themselves and each other. If the group is set up right, one of you will be a comedy maven, another a devotee of horror, etc. Maybe one knows a producer who can't help him but can help you. If you don't know of any groups, check out the Net or start one yourself.

> **Become An Expert** — You like movies so much, well start reviewing movies. Do it in your local paper or online. The career of director/writer Rod Lurie started in this way. Likewise François Truffaut. At some point, someone realized these two guys knew what they were talking about and gave them a chance to make their own films. By becoming critics, they had a platform from which to be heard. And when the time came to put their money where their mouths were, they were ready with their own scripts and projects.

> **Come to Los Angeles** — Whether you come out for a week or a lifetime, L.A. is where the business is, so what are you doing living in Dubuque? If I were starting all over again, I would come to L.A. and get any job, preferably one as a script reader.

I would read as many scripts and make as many contacts as I could while keeping my screenwriting going on the side. If I could only come out for a week, I would be available for as many meetings as possible with producers; industry get-togethers at SAG, DGA, WGA; and be ready with my bio, business card, sample scripts, treatments, and photo so they remember my face. What's stopping you?

> **You.com** – Though I have not tried this route — not yet anyway — how about starting a Web site all about you and your career? Put up your photo and bio. List scripts in progress, treatments, and sample pages that are available to download, and even details of deals in progress with referrals to those you're in business with (with their permission, of course). You.com is a great thing to reference and put on a business card. You want to know who I am? Check out my Web site.

DON'T TRY THIS AT HOME...

Knowing what to do is as important as knowing what *not* to do. Here are a few things that people advise that I think are less beneficial. Remember the key ingredient in marketing yourself is to meet people — face to face if possible, so the following seem like busy work to me:

> **Screenplay Contests** – This is something I'm going to get skewered for but I just have to say it: I think screenwriting contests are a colossal waste of time. It's a trend that's been springing up of late, and many writers live and die by the results, waiting by the phone or the mail box to see if they made it to the top 10% tier — whatever that is. I have one word for such activity: Stop. It means just about zero to any agent or producer with anything real going on. It's nice if you like contests; to me, it's an echo chamber. Do they give you any

money for these contests? Are they going to make your film with an A-list cast? No! ! I haven't seen one script from one contest get turned into a Tom Cruise movie, have you? And we are here to sell our scripts to the likes of B.O. stars like him. Are we together on this? Good!

On the other hand... there are some contests that sponsor panels of experts who have actually sold to or work for the majors. These professionals can offer invaluable learning and networking opportunities. So if you must enter a contest, you have a job to do first: Read carefully. Ask questions. Seek out the legitimate, the ones with high-level pros who will be available at panels and/or seminars. If they're not associated with the contest, you shouldn't be either.

> **Stupid Screenwriter Tricks** — However clever we think we are, sometimes we go too far in our enthusiasm. We are creative people and think everyone will get it — well, they don't. Stunts don't work. Lame attempts to get attention don't work. Here are some other don'ts: Don't package yourself in a big crate and mail yourself to William Morris. Don't take out a full-page advertisement in *Variety* with your picture and phone number with the slogan: Will Write for Food. Don't have your picture taken with a cut-out photo of your favorite movie star and send to him autographed with the phrase: We should be in business together! And whatever you do, don't threaten to leap off the Hollywood sign as leverage to get someone to read your screenplay. It's been done, babe, it's been done.

SOME MARKETING HITS AND MISSES

I would be remiss in my advice on how to sell yourself and your screenplay if I didn't give you examples of things that I've done

— some worked and some didn't — to get my screenplays sold. I have tried it all. Take these for what they're worth and try them at your peril.

In the area of "specialty pitches," I can tell you some good stories, including doing so well in one meeting with my longtime friend and co-writer, the fabulously funny Tracey Jackson, that producer David Permut flew us to New York the next day to pitch our idea to Howard Stern. You hear of these amazing presentations; some producers and writers are better at it and more successful than others. And they're certainly fun to know about. One of the best at it is producer David Kirschner (*Chucky*, *An American Tail*). David has made it his personal specialty to be able to line up pitch meetings at the top studios and really put on a show. When David had the rights to the '50s TV series *Leave it to Beaver*, and went in to Universal to pitch the movie, he brought a surprise guest. During David's pitch, there was a knock at the door and Barbara Billingsley, the original Mrs. Cleaver, came in to serve executives milk and cookies. David took his pitch to exactly one studio.

Deal!

For his pitch to Disney to sell the Bette Midler movie *Hocus Pocus*, David created a spooky, effects-laden coven complete with actresses dressed as witches to enhance the mood. In this atmosphere, David wove his own selling spell. By the time he was done, the Disney execs were bewitched.

Deal!

Maybe the king of the logline working today, the man with a thousand pitches at his command, is producer Bob Kosberg. Bob makes a sale or two every month. He's amazing. Working with writers on ideas of his own, and theirs too, he can conceptualize better than anyone in the business and can weed out the clunkers from the winners with lightning speed. Every time he walks into the room, he has a new one to pitch.

Deal!

I, too, have done specialty pitches. The one I remember most was a hilarious failure. My first partner, Howard Burkons, and I had a movie idea called *B.M.O.C.*, which was basically *Tootsie* on a college campus. Howard volunteered to do the pitch dressed as a woman, in full makeup and outfit, just to get the idea across that it was possible. And as great as Howard looks in a dress, we did not sell *B.M.O.C.*

No deal!

Howard did, however, get asked out at Disney.

I have had success with specialty marketing. During the spec sale frenzy of the early '90s, the buzz surrounding any virgin screenplay that was on the block for sale was huge. Word that a new script was going "out to the town" started days and weeks beforehand. The script was **tracked** by development execs, and their bosses often yelled and screamed demanding to be put on the list.

In this atmosphere, making your script sale special became a fad. For the sale of a script called *Ticking Man*, ticking clocks with alarms all set to the same time were sent out to executives prior to getting the script. The alarms went off all over town at the moment messengers arrived with the script. Talk about building and paying off tension!

The *Nuclear Family* Script Containment Unit (1992)

When Jim Haggin and I were ready to send out our spec script, *Nuclear Family*, we decided to package it in artistically designed "radioactive script containment units," into which we stuck the script as our way of setting the mood. We made 20 of these from materials we bought at an Army surplus store; only the most special producers were on the list to get one. After clearing this special delivery with the security gate at every studio (these things looked so much like a bomb we didn't want any false red alerts), the send-out was coordinated by our agent, Hilary, as messengers delivered our script containment units in a flurry of activity all over town. By the time the day was over, Jeffery Katzenberg at Disney and Steven Spielberg at Amblin had personally gotten on the phone to make a bid.

A year or so later, Colby Carr and I stuffed several dozen kid's backpacks with a million dollars in play money for Hilary to send out *Blank Check* — basically the storyline of the script in a finely made, 3-D souvenir.

Blank Check backpacks (1993)

Each of these specialty presentations resulted in a million-dollar sale. And headlines in *Variety* the next day noted the marketing innovations and the bidding war both inspired. For our part, we always devised these because we were genuinely enthusiastic about our script, and wanted to get the reader in the mood — just like a good marketing campaign gets a nationwide audience in the mood to see a summer blockbuster. It's a truism that the easiest people to sell are salesmen. I am a sucker for a great campaign of any kind. And so are the executives in Hollywood. They like a good show as much as the next person and are more likely to applaud the effort. Besides, we had a ball doing it!

Of course this kind of marketing is oldhat now. No one does these little tricks anymore. It's doubtful this type of selling will come back. Too many scripts that were bought did not get made and the spec script craze has died. Studios nowadays don't like to be that out of control when it comes to bidding on scripts, so they don't get into bidding wars as often or as eagerly as they used to. But it was fun while it lasted! Who knows what the next innovative tactic will be — via the Internet maybe? — to get the attention that will set your script apart in the crowd. After all, this is a business that still likes special effects, surprise, and showmanship.

IT IS WHAT IT IS

Okay. Last words on the entire subject. I am a little teary about ending this book. It's been fun to write and I hope that in some way it's been helpful to you. I have been honored to be a part of this business from the time I was a very little kid. I've had great adventures, lots of truly creative moments, and met some of the most amazing people. It's been a great ride.

I've also been faced with terrible self-doubt and self-recrimination. You get bumped in this business, and want to throw in the towel from time to time. But if it's in your blood, like it's in mine, you learn to persevere. And you get as much education from failure as success. If you keep trying and stay focused, you can have any prize in the firmament. All you have to do is keep working at it, have a great attitude, and know that today just might be "the day."

Right before Colby Carr and I ever sent a script out, gave it to our agent, or to the producer, we had a little saying to take the sting away. We knew that we had done our best. With Colby, as with all my writing partners, we work hard for the money. And we are harder on ourselves than any critic could possibly be. Just before we dropped that script in the mail or surrendered it to the messenger, Colby and I would say: "It is what it is." That phrase means that certain artistic projects, when combined with the need for those projects to make a profit, are penned in by demands that you must meet. If you meet them satisfactorily, if you've done your job, if you've covered yourself from every angle, if you've met every criteria and done so creatively, that's all you can do. You've done your best.

The rest is fate.

It is what it is.

The business is what it is too. And while I often rebel against it, or try to bullhead my way past it, there's no way around it. "They," meaning the people who run the studios and make the decisions, do all kinds of things that drive creative people like us mad, but they are in charge. Yes, they buy into someone's "heat" and ignore others, more talented, who are unknown. They often don't read scripts thoroughly. And they are more interested in the headline and the opportunity you represent than your growth as an artist.

But that's the nature of business.

It is what it is.

You must find a life within the confines of "It is what it is." This is where your skills as a bullhead will save both you and your sanity. And while I've made fun of this trait throughout this book, I do it as a means of challenging you to be more so: Whatever you do, don't stop being a bullhead. The powers-that-be can take away a lot of things. They can buy your script and fire you, or rewrite it into oblivion, but they can't take away your ability to get up off the mat and come back swinging — better and smarter than you were before.

Most of all, you must try to find the fun in everything you write. Because having fun lets you know you're on the right track. So that when you write those two dazzling words, FADE IN:, the hundredth time, you're as excited as you were when you wrote them the first.

GLOSSARY

FREQUENT TERMS IN USE IN THE 310 AREA CODE

ARC — This denotes the changes a character experiences as tracked from the beginning, through the middle, to the end of a screenplay. Most often heard in development meetings as in: "What's the arc of the hero?" and "Are these characters arcing enough?" To which you think to yourself: "What is the arc of my patience to sit here and listen to this?"

AT THE END OF THE DAY — A phrase used by agents and managers to indicate they are about to give you bad news, i.e., "We love your script and think it would be *great* for Julia, but at the end of the day does she really need to do a musical set in the Middle Ages?" Also when you are most likely to be called by said agent or manager with this bad news.

BLACK HOLES — These are the spots in your beat sheet, step outline, or places on The Board that you have no idea how to fill with story. Looking at black holes will cause you to wonder how you got into the business. You could have gone to law school or joined the Army but no, you had to do this!

BLOCK COMEDY — A low budget, domestically oriented, family film. It is so low tech and requires so few company moves, you can shoot it on the backlot — as they did with *The 'Burbs*. I first heard this term at Disney when we were discussing a script we had sold to them called *Poker Night*. And it all takes place — on the block. "We want more of these," said the executive in charge. "You know, a block comedy!" I had never heard the term before. It may just be his term, but I like it, and now it's mine.

BOARD, THE — A corkboard, blackboard, or artist's notebook that divides a screenplay-in-progress into four equal parts: Act One, the first half of Act Two, the second half of Act Two, and Act Three. It is the workout space where, using index cards, pushpins, colored Pentels, etc., you can try your best ideas and see what they look like, and then begin to winnow them down. If done right, you'll end up with 40 scenes that make a movie, all laid out neatly on The Board in your office or workroom... along with blood, sweat, and tears.

BREAKING THE FOURTH WALL — A filmmaker's inside joke that makes the audience realize they are watching a film. The fourth wall is an invisible one that allows the audience to look into the lives of characters on stage. And breaking it lets the characters, essentially, look back. This "takes you out of the story." Sometimes it works, as when Woody Allen speaks to the audience in *Annie Hall*. But most times it does not, as when Robin Williams "breaks character" (like in *Aladdin*).

BOOSTER ROCKET — There are spots in any screenplay that are potentially dull stretches. Usually these are found right after "big moments" like after the Act One break and sections where the action is petering out, like at the end of Act Two. This is a time to stick in a booster rocket to get us past these spots. John Candy in *Home Alone* is the classic example. The tale of a Mom (Catherine O'Hara) getting home to her child is starting to drag around the end of Act Two. So when John Candy and his polka-band cohorts show up, it's just what the script doctor ordered. Another booster rocket character is the manicurist in *Legally Blonde*. She arrives just when we're growing weary of Elle Woods' law school saga, just after the break into Act Two of that screenplay. Both these characters rocket us past these potential slow spots.

CALLBACKS — Bits, images, character traits, and metaphors that are set up in Act One and then recalled later in the movie. Often the callback explains what that obvious set-up was about. In *Back to the Future*, the flier upon which Marty McFly's girlfriend writes "I Love You" reminds Marty of the clock tower and the electric storm in 1955 that he needs to power his DeLorean back to 1985. This is a nice callback. Other callbacks are less plot-oriented and remind us of a character's growth, harkening the past to show change or to re-emphasize a joke by reminding us of its origins.

CREDIT JUMPER — You have sold your script to the studio. Then, after your contracted rewrite, you are fired. And when the movie goes into production, and you are sent drafts of the rewritten version of your script, you are suddenly appalled to find that... it's been altered!! Often in stupid ways: Your hero Bob is now named Carl. Instead of a Pontiac, he drives a Buick. Congratulations, you've been victimized by a credit jumper, a guy or gal who is gunning for writing credit on your movie and thinks by making these tweaks it will become his or her own. This is why we have WGA credit-arbitration committees to decide who did what. The advantage of writing on spec and being the originator now becomes clear. You have more rights than the average credit jumper. It's up to you to say why specifically this is still your script. And you must! (Isn't Hollywood a great town?)

EXPOSITION — Give me the facts, ma'am, just the facts, but please do it in a way that won't put me to sleep. Thus, exposition — like annoying plot details, heist plans, and backstories — can't be just laid out, it must be entertainingly told by crafty screenwriters. To "bury" said exposition is to deal with it in a way that is not deadly dull. The masters of the craft make these irritating facts and figures go down as easily as a spoonful of Maypo.

FIRST REEL — During the era of silent films, film reels were 10 minutes long, thus the end of the first reel was 10 minutes into the movie. Flash forward to Joel Silver, genius producer of such action pictures as *Die Hard* and *Matrix*, who wisely suggests that you have a "whammy" or a big action set piece at the end of every "reel." The First Reel still denotes the first 10 minutes of a movie and *I* suggest it be used to introduce every A-story character.

FOUR-QUADRANT PICTURE — The big magilla. The whole ball of wax. The mother lode. Audience-wise, if you have a four-quadrant hit, you have won the lottery. The four quadrants are Men Over 25, Men Under 25, Women Over 25, and Woman Under 25. If you can draw audience from all those quadrants, you are guaranteeing yourself a hit. Why isn't every movie a four-quadrant movie? Everyone targets different groups for different reasons. As I write today, the single most desirable group is Men Under 25. Most movies are geared to them because they go, with or without their girlfriends. They are more likely to bring others to their movies than they are likely to be brought to other movies. They are the leading indicators of "who goes." This may change, but it explains the movie selections at the mall on any given weekend. Have a complaint no one's making movies for you? That's why. But for the spec screenwriters of the world trying to make a sale, this is invaluable information.

GENRE — After we get past the main headings of, say, Comedy and Drama, genre breaks down into more specific groupings. If it's a comedy, then what type of comedy is it? Is it a family film, romantic comedy, spoof, or teen comedy? If it's a drama, is it an action, romance, thriller, or horror movie? Each of these is a genre that has its own rules, history, and expectations from an audience. And though the fusion of different genres is now *de rigueur* in short-attention-span Hollywood (Ron Howard's *The Missing* is a Gothic/Western), I suggest one genre per movie, please. Any more and I personally don't know what it is, or why I go see it.

HIGH CONCEPT — No one knows exactly how to explain this unwieldy term. I know. I've asked. What is "high" about a high concept? The term is fuzzy regarding what it's trying to describe. Also, I've asked about the exact place and time this phrase was coined and have come up short. That said, we know what it means: *Die Hard* is a high concept movie; *English Patient* is not. *Miss Congeniality* is a high concept movie; *Under The Tuscan Sun* is not. Mostly you can divide it into American (high concept) and European (non-high concept), which also explains why American movies do well and European movies do not — well, everywhere but Europe. I advise you to write as high a high concept movie as you can the first time out, and if you know of the exact terminology or origin of the term "high concept" e-mail me... I'll be in Europe.

HOOK — Ah, *le hook!* This is the encapsulation of a movie, be it displayed on the poster or in the logline, which grabs your attention and makes you want to run, not walk, to the theatre. And when mentioned in *Variety*, it is the thing that makes you hit yourself on the head and say: "Why didn't *I* think of that?" Like Proust's *madeleine*, the hook must blossom in your mind with possibility and "hook" you into wanting more — thus the name. It is a simple mental picture that promises fun and gives you enough of a peek into the storyline that you can see the potential. A good hook is gold for this reason: It works on anyone who hears it, be it agent, producer, studio head, or ticket buyer. A good hook answers: "What is it?"

INACTIVE HERO — What lays there like a lox on a plate? Who can't be bothered to get up out of his chair and go answer the door? Why, the inactive hero, of course. And since the very definition of a hero is to be proactive, the inactive kind must not be a very good thing. Heroes seek, strive, and reach for the stars; they don't wait for the phone to ring. So if your hero is inactive, tell him to get off the dime!

IN PLAY — When we say that someone is in play, we mean that they have so much "heat" and are so "desirable" that the news they are looking for new representation makes the town jump up and down with hysteric joy. For actors who want to leave their agents, for directors and producers who have eschewed their studios when their on-the-lot deal ends and are looking for a new "home," being in play means lots of buzz, money, and attention is about to be paid. If you are a screenwriter, this term does not apply to you. While you very well may be "in play," to the town it just means you are "available."

LOGLINE OR ONE-LINE — A logline is the one- or two-sentence description of your movie that tells us what it is. It must contain a type of hero (that means a type of person plus an adjective that describes him), the antagonist (ditto), and the hero's primal goal. It must have irony, and it must bloom in our brains with potential. A good logline is the coin of the realm in Hollywood and can be traded like currency with those who appreciate it.

MAJOR TURNS — The break into Act One, the midpoint, and the break into Act Three are the major turns of a script. These are conveniently found at the end of each horizontal row on The Board. These are also the places that need to be paid the most attention. In a pitch you will hang your hat on these major turns and if you're lucky, executives will remember one of them. But you must always have them nailed before you pitch and before you can "beat out" a screenplay.

ONE-SHEET — This is the old timer's phrase for "the poster." I have no idea where this term originated, only that it has to do with printing size. A one-sheet is the broad sheet that shows the stars, title, and tone of the film. A good one is gold. One-sheets sell DVDs in the aftermarket, too.

ON THE NOSE a.k.a. A Little Too on the Nose — This is one of my favorite development executive phrases, uttered when a suggestion is obvious, unfunny, or something "we've seen before." Instead of saying "That's obvious, unfunny, and something we've seen before," they say, "It feels a little on the nose." You, who have been up all night trying not to be "on the nose," now think of this as a target suggestion.

PAGE ONE — "It's a Page One!" This is the despairing cry of the development executive who has been handed a script with a good idea and maybe some good characters and little else. It means that some poor schmuck will be assigned to give this a "page one rewrite." It is the equivalent of an auto body repairman telling the owner of a damaged car: "It's totaled."

PRE-SOLD FRANCHISE — When a book, comic book, cartoon, or old TV series has a built-in group of fans, it is considered to be a pre-sold franchise. It presumes that a certain number of people are already "sold" on the property and will turn up to see it when the movie comes out. This is not always the case — just ask the producers of *The Avengers* and *The League of Extraordinary Gentlemen*. Still, having any group of potential ticket buyers aware of your movie before you go into production is a head start. Even obscure beginnings, like the comic book that spawned *Men In Black*, got started from the belief that even a small fan base will get buzz started with moviegoers. But a pre-sold franchise is also something a spec screenwriter is not likely to own. That should not stop you from creating your own franchises, and I encourage you to create the biggest franchise possible.

PRIMAL — What is basic about a story, a character's goal, or a movie premise is its relation to our inner drives as human beings. Stories of survival, sex, hunger, and revenge connote immediate interest on our part. We will stop and look when these themes are presented to us. We can't help it. We *have* to look. It's primal. To you, the screenwriter, this means you must ground every action and story in its primal-ness. When characters are not acting like human beings, when they are not being driven primally, odds are you are testing the patience of the audience. To ask "Is it primal?" is to ask "Is this relevant to a caveman?" The answer must be: Yes!

PROMISE OF THE PREMISE — The premise of a movie, its "What is it?", can only be proven to be satisfying when we see it in action. What is fun, catchy, or hooks our interest about a movie's poster must be paid off once we get inside the theater. If it is not paid off, we the audience will consider it to be a bad experience. We will feel cheated. The promise of the premise are those scenes or scene sequences that exploit the premise to its maximum and are usually found in the fun and games section (pages 30-55) of a screenplay. This is the point where we understand fully what this movie is about. This is why we bought our tickets.

RESIDUALS — Lovely lime-green envelopes come through the mail to the homes of lucky screenwriters on a quarterly basis. We know what's inside: money! That explains the desire to get a movie made, for its every appearance on TV, every VHS or DVD sale, every foreign manifestation will be tracked by the WGA Residual Department and result in... more residuals! And the amounts are nothing to sneeze at: I have earned over $100,000 in residuals in my career for two movies. And the checks haven't stopped coming. Get enough movies in production and you will be showered in these bonus checks for the rest of your natural life.

RUNNING GAGS — As opposed to callbacks, which are reminders of plot and character moments in Act One that are paid off later, running gags are repeating themes, character tics, or bits that are interspersed throughout a movie or a screenplay. As an audience, our appreciation for these gags grows with each use because we feel smart for remembering them and feel more a part of the story because of it. If a character is set up as liking coffee, then whenever he or she walks into a restaurant and orders coffee — we love it! It's nothing. But we laugh with recognition that we *know* this character. Running gags can be found in both dramas and comedies as repeating jokes we notice and remember. Note: The running gag must be given a twist later in the film when a character, by now ready to change, goes into a café and orders... tea.

SET PIECE — A set piece is a stand-alone action scene or sequence. It stands alone in that it does less to move the plot forward or enhance our idea of who the characters are as it exploits the possibilities of the situation or the premise of a movie. Because of this, set pieces are disposable and interchangeable. A "chase scene" that takes place on a freeway and does little, in itself, to move the plot forward, can be set in a supermarket, playground, or racetrack. That's a set piece — one that can be dropped or changed within the confines of a studio's slashing of the budget, a director's "vision," or a star's dislike of chase scenes on freeways.

SIX THINGS THAT NEED FIXING — This is my term. And I use it all the time. It is defined as the list of a hero's minor character flaws, enemies and rivals that bully him, and a wish list that — if we like the hero enough, and think he deserves help — get "fixed" later in the film. I personally find myself going back and forth between Act One (set-up) and Act Two or Three (pay-off) and adding things to the list as I go. We as an audience like to see the Six Things That Need Fixing get paid off later in the script — the more the merrier. It's thoroughly enjoyable to see those pay-offs. But you have to put the flaw in there in the beginning to make the pay-off work.

STAKES ARE RAISED — This is a term that is frequently heard in development meetings. Also known as the "ticking clock" or the "midpoint bump," it means the raising of the level of tension.

Suddenly from out of nowhere at the midpoint, some new thing — an even bigger and more unexpected thing than we've seen before, and one that seems insurmountable — becomes a problem for our hero. You must be sure the stakes are raised at the midpoint to give the hero new challenges and lead him to his ultimate win.

STRUCTURE — After "concept," the single most important quality of a good screenplay is its structure. Very often a producer or executive will applaud the idea, love the writing, and toss out the script because the structure is a mess. They cannot see how the movie is organized. And without that, they often don't know what it is. Good structure is one of several prime components that will help sell your script — and is the easiest to learn. So learn it! It is part of the language we use to communicate with each other in development meetings, so you must be fluent.

SUBTEXT — That part of a scene, sequence, or screenplay that lies beneath the surface and is in fact its real meaning. The subtext of an argument between a soon-to-be-divorced couple about buying apples is not whether they choose Macintosh or Pink Lady but the fact that the couple is having problems — and an argument about produce proves it! Do not hit us over the head with what's really going on, it's much more subtle — and better screenwritin' — to hide the meaning. It's not what they're talking about, it's what they're not talking about that makes these moments so rich.

THEMATIC PREMISE — What is this movie about? Yes, even the silliest monster movie or most spastic comedy has to be "about something." If it's not, it's not a good movie. In essence every good movie is a debate about the pros and the cons of a particular point of view. It is a question raised and answered by the movie. The place to stick that question is up front, loud and clear. It is frequently spoken by a minor character to the hero in the form of a question early on, like on page 5, and sets the debate into motion that will be proven, one way or the other, in the course of the movie. This question and debate is the movie's thematic premise.

THESIS, ANTITHESIS, SYNTHESIS a.k.a. Act One, Act Two, and Act Three — Thesis, antithesis, and synthesis describe the thematic progression of the hero's journey. In Act One, the hero's world is set up. In Act Two that world is turned on its head; it is the upside down version of what he left behind. But by mastering this surreal new world, the hero gains the knowledge to combine what was and its opposite to form a synthesis of everything he has learned. That synthesis occurs in Act Three. It is not enough for the hero to survive the journey; he must transform his world in order to truly be great.

TRACKING — If you have a hot script, either on its way out to the town or about to be, odds are it will be "tracked" by development executives who closely follow its progress. They have even set up an inter-studio Intranet to talk to each other about scripts and whether or not the script is worth the effort of pursuing for purchase. Based on the concept, track record of the writer, and word of mouth, the script will be considered either hot or not. Sometimes, executives will try to outfox each other with mis-information on a hot script, but this sort of maneuver can backfire on them next time. This current tracking system is one of several reasons, mostly economic, that the spec sale frenzy has ended in Hollywood. Tracking scripts in this way cuts down on the chances of any of the studios or their buyers getting burned.

WHIFF OF DEATH — The added extra bonus found in the All Is Lost point on page 75 of a well-structured screenplay. It is that very special moment where something metaphorically, or actually, dies. And since this is the place where the mentor bites the big one, the moment when best friends and allies you thought looked sick now kick the bucket, and the spot where Spot is removed, this is the perfect place to put such story beats. The All Is Lost point is rife with the whiff of death because it marks the end of the world as is and the beginning of a new world the hero will create from this seeming end.

+/- — This symbol indicates the emotional change of a good scene. I first heard about this from Robert McKee. He believes that every scene should mark a sea change like this, going from one emotional extreme to another. And he's right. If you think of each scene as a mini-movie, you must have a *before* snapshot and an *after* snapshot to show this change. Deciding what the emotional shift in each of your scenes involves is the key element in making that scene a success. When I am using index cards and my corkboard to work out the structure of a movie, I mark each card with this symbol and make sure I know what the emotional change is in each scene.

>< — This symbol represents the conflict in each scene. When the scene starts, who has a goal, who's in the way, who wins? These questions can be boiled down into one neat statement using this symbol to denote who's up against whom. Don't start a scene unless you have figured out who your players are and what they want.

ABOUT THE AUTHOR

Blake Snyder joined the family business at age 8, working as a voice talent for his father, Emmy-winning TV producer, Ken Snyder (*Roger Ramjet*, *Big Blue Marble*).

Blake began his career writing for the Disney TV series, *Kids Incorporated*, penning 13 episodes before turning to writing spec screenplays full time. Before long, a trade journal noted that Blake had become "one of Hollywood's most successful spec screenwriters."

Blake has sold many original scripts and pitches to the major studios, including two million-dollar sales (one to Steven Spielberg), and has had two films produced. *Stop! Or My Mom Will Shoot*, *Third Grade*, and *Nuclear Family* sold to Universal; *Poker Night*, *Drips*, *Blank Check*, and *Herbie Comes Home* for Disney; *How I Joined the CIA* and *Big, Ugly Baby!* sold to Fox Family TV; and *Alienators* to Total Film Group.

Blake made his 13th spec script sale, *Granny*, in 2004 and is currently working with production partner, Classic Media, to get *Roger Ramjet* made into a major motion picture.

He lives in Beverly Hills, California.

SAVE THE CAT!™ GOES TO THE MOVIES
THE SCREENWRITER'S GUIDE
TO EVERY STORY EVER TOLD

BLAKE SNYDER

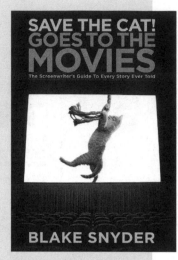

In the long-awaited sequel to his surprise bestseller, *Save the Cat!*, author and screenwriter Blake Snyder returns to form in a fast-paced follow-up that proves why his is the most talked-about approach to screenwriting in years. In the perfect companion piece to his first book, Snyder delivers even more insider's information gleaned from a 20-year track record as "one of Hollywood's most successful spec screenwriters," giving you the clues to write *your* movie.

Designed for screenwriters, novelists, and movie fans, this book gives readers the key breakdowns of the 50 most instructional movies from the past 30 years. From *M*A*S*H* to *Crash*, from *Alien* to *Saw*, from *10* to *Eternal Sunshine of the Spotless Mind*, Snyder reveals how screenwriters who came before you tackled the same challenges you are facing with the film you want to write — or the one you are currently working on.

Writing a "rom-com"? Check out the "Buddy Love" chapter for a "beat for beat" dissection of *When Harry Met Sally...* plus references to 10 other great romantic comedies that will make your story sing.

Want to execute a great mystery? Go to the "Whydunit" section and learn about the "dark turn" that's essential to the heroes of *All the President's Men*, *Blade Runner*, *Fargo* and hip noir *Brick* — and see why ALL good stories, whether a Hollywood blockbuster or a Sundance award winner, follow the same rules of structure outlined in Snyder's breakthrough method.

If you want to sell your script and create a movie that pleases most audiences most of the time, the odds increase if you reference Snyder's checklists and see what makes 50 films tick. After all, both executives and audiences respond to the same elements good writers seek to master. They want to know the type of story they signed on for, and whether it's structured in a way that satisfies everyone. It's what they're looking for. And now, it's what you can deliver.

BLAKE SNYDER, besides selling million-dollar scripts to both Disney and Spielberg, is still "one of Hollywood's most successful spec screenwriters," having made another spec sale in 2006. An in-demand scriptcoach and seminar and workshop leader, Snyder provides information for writers through his website, *www.blakesnyder.com*.

$24.95 · 270 PAGES · ORDER NUMBER 75RLS · ISBN: 9781932907353

THE WRITER'S JOURNEY – 3RD EDITION
MYTHIC STRUCTURE FOR WRITERS

CHRISTOPHER VOGLER

BEST SELLER
OVER 180,000 COPIES SOLD!

See why this book has become an international best seller and a true classic. *The Writer's Journey* explores the powerful relationship between mythology and storytelling in a clear, concise style that's made it required reading for movie executives, screenwriters, playwrights, scholars, and fans of pop culture all over the world.

Both fiction and nonfiction writers will discover a set of useful myth-inspired storytelling paradigms (i.e., "The Hero's Journey") and step-by-step guidelines to plot and character development. Based on the work of Joseph Campbell, *The Writer's Journey* is a must for all writers interested in further developing their craft.

The updated and revised third edition provides new insights and observations from Vogler's ongoing work on mythology's influence on stories, movies, and man himself.

"This book is like having the smartest person in the story meeting come home with you and whisper what to do in your ear as you write a screenplay. Insight for insight, step for step, Chris Vogler takes us through the process of connecting theme to story and making a script come alive."
> – Lynda Obst, Producer, *Sleepless in Seattle, How to Lose a Guy in 10 Days*;
> Author, *Hello, He Lied*

"This is a book about the stories we write, and perhaps more importantly, the stories we live. It is the most influential work I have yet encountered on the art, nature, and the very purpose of storytelling."
> – Bruce Joel Rubin, Screenwriter, *Stuart Little 2, Deep Impact,*
> *Ghost, Jacob's Ladder*

CHRISTOPHER VOGLER is a veteran story consultant for major Hollywood film companies and a respected teacher of filmmakers and writers around the globe. He has influenced the stories of movies from *The Lion King* to *Fight Club* to *The Thin Red Line* and most recently wrote the first installment of *Ravenskull*, a Japanese-style manga or graphic novel. He is the executive producer of the feature film *P.S. Your Cat is Dead* and writer of the animated feature *Jester Till*.

$26.95 · 448 PAGES · ORDER NUMBER 76RLS · ISBN: 9781932907360

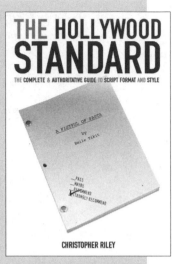

FILM & VIDEO BOOKS

SCREENWRITING | WRITING

And the Best Screenplay Goes to... | Dr. Linda Seger | $26.95

Archetypes for Writers | Jennifer Van Bergen | $22.95

Cinematic Storytelling | Jennifer Van Sijll | $24.95

Could It Be a Movie? | Christina Hamlett | $26.95

Creating Characters | Marisa D'Vari | $26.95

Crime Writer's Reference Guide, The | Martin Roth | $20.95

Deep Cinema | Mary Trainor-Brigham | $19.95

Elephant Bucks | Sheldon Bull | $24.95

Fast, Cheap & Written That Way | John Gaspard | $26.95

Hollywood Standard, The | Christopher Riley | $18.95

I Could've Written a Better Movie than That! | Derek Rydall | $26.95

Inner Drives | Pamela Jaye Smith | $26.95

Joe Leydon's Guide to Essential Movies You Must See | Joe Leydon | $24.95

Moral Premise, The | Stanley D. Williams, Ph.D. | $24.95

Myth and the Movies | Stuart Voytilla | $26.95

Power of the Dark Side, The | Pamela Jaye Smith | $22.95

Psychology for Screenwriters | William Indick, Ph.D. | $26.95

Rewrite | Paul Chitlik | $16.95

Romancing the A-List | Christopher Keane | $18.95

Save the Cat! | Blake Snyder | $19.95

Save the Cat! Goes to the Movies | Blake Snyder | $24.95

Screenwriting 101 | Neill D. Hicks | $16.95

Screenwriting for Teens | Christina Hamlett | $18.95

Script-Selling Game, The | Kathie Fong Yoneda | $16.95

Stealing Fire From the Gods, 2nd Edition | James Bonnet | $26.95

Way of Story, The | Catherine Ann Jones | $22.95

What Are You Laughing At? | Brad Schreiber | $19.95

Writer's Journey, – 3rd Edition, The | Christopher Vogler | $26.95

Writer's Partner, The | Martin Roth | $24.95

Writing the Action Adventure Film | Neill D. Hicks | $14.95

Writing the Comedy Film | Stuart Voytilla & Scott Petri | $14.95

Writing the Killer Treatment | Michael Halperin | $14.95

Writing the Second Act | Michael Halperin | $19.95

Writing the Thriller Film | Neill D. Hicks | $14.95

Writing the TV Drama Series – 2nd Edition | Pamela Douglas | $26.95

Your Screenplay Sucks! | William M. Akers | $19.95

FILMMAKING

Film School | Richard D. Pepperman | $24.95

Power of Film, The | Howard Suber | $27.95

PITCHING

Perfect Pitch – 2nd Edition, The | Ken Rotcop | $19.95

Selling Your Story in 60 Seconds | Michael Hauge | $12.95

SHORTS

Filmmaking for Teens | Troy Lanier & Clay Nichols | $18.95

Ultimate Filmmaker's Guide to Short Films, The | Kim Adelman | $16.95

BUDGET | PRODUCTION MGMT

Film & Video Budgets, 4th Updated Edition | Deke Simon & Michael Wiese | $26.95

Film Production Management 101 | Deborah S. Patz | $39.95

DIRECTING | VISUALIZATION

Animation Unleashed | Ellen Besen | $26.95

Citizen Kane Crash Course in Cinematography | David Worth | $19.95

Directing Actors | Judith Weston | $26.95

Directing Feature Films | Mark Travis | $26.95

Fast, Cheap & Under Control | John Gaspard | $26.95

Film Directing: Cinematic Motion, 2nd Edition | Steven D. Katz | $27.95

Film Directing: Shot by Shot | Steven D. Katz | $27.95

Film Director's Intuition, The | Judith Weston | $26.95

First Time Director | Gil Bettman | $27.95

From Word to Image | Marcie Begleiter | $26.95

I'll Be in My Trailer! | John Badham & Craig Modderno | $26.95

Master Shots | Christopher Kenworthy | $24.95

Setting Up Your Scenes | Richard D. Pepperman | $24.95

Setting Up Your Shots, 2nd Edition | Jeremy Vineyard | $22.95

Working Director, The | Charles Wilkinson | $22.95

DIGITAL | DOCUMENTARY | SPECIAL

Digital Filmmaking 101, 2nd Edition | Dale Newton & John Gaspard | $26.95

Digital Moviemaking 3.0 | Scott Billups | $24.95

Digital Video Secrets | Tony Levelle | $26.95

Greenscreen Made Easy | Jeremy Hanke & Michele Yamazaki | $19.95

Producing with Passion | Dorothy Fadiman & Tony Levelle | $22.95

Special Effects | Michael Slone | $31.95

EDITING

Cut by Cut | Gael Chandler | $35.95

Cut to the Chase | Bobbie O'Steen | $24.95

Eye is Quicker, The | Richard D. Pepperman | $27.95

Invisible Cut, The | Bobbie O'Steen | $28.95

SOUND | DVD | CAREER

Complete DVD Book, The | Chris Gore & Paul J. Salamoff | $26.95

Costume Design 101 | Richard La Motte | $19.95

Hitting Your Mark – 2nd Edition | Steve Carlson | $22.95

Sound Design | David Sonnenschein | $19.95

Sound Effects Bible, The | Ric Viers | $26.95

Storyboarding 101 | James Fraioli | $19.95

There's No Business Like Soul Business | Derek Rydall | $22.95

FINANCE | MARKETING | FUNDING

Art of Film Funding, The | Carole Lee Dean | $26.95

Complete Independent Movie Marketing Handbook, The | Mark Steven Bosko | $39.95

Independent Film and Videomakers Guide – 2nd Edition, The | Michael Wiese | $29.95

Independent Film Distribution | Phil Hall | $26.95

Shaking the Money Tree, 2nd Edition | Morrie Warshawski | $26.95

OUR FILMS

Dolphin Adventures: DVD | Michael Wiese and Hardy Jones | $24.95

On the Edge of a Dream | Michael Wiese | $16.95

Sacred Sites of the Dalai Lamas– DVD, The | Documentary by Michael Wiese | $24.95

Hardware Wars: DVD | Written and Directed by Ernie Fosselius | $14.95